A Few Who Made a Difference

A Few Who Made a Difference

The World War II Teams of the
Military Intelligence Service

Karl W. Abt

VANTAGE PRESS
New York

Contents

Acknowledgments

Over the years since 1944-45, I managed to keep track of both Henry Schuster and Jan Polivka of IPW Team 97. Then, in 1997, using a new computer, I located three more surviving members of the team in the telephone listings on the Internet. They were Henry Griesman, Paul Seiden and Walter Waller. Our first team reunion occurred in 1998 in White Plains, New York. When we rediscovered our kinship with one another and realized that the remaining years would not be many, we met every year, with our wives along to share the good times. Subsequent reunions took place in San Francisco, Chicago, Savannah in Georgia and Asheville in North Carolina. Along the way, we lost Walter's wife Lee in 1999 and Jan Polivka in 2001, preceded by his wife Helen. This narrative, however, captures the recollection of the events in 1944 and 1945 from all the team's members.

In addition to Team 97, I was able to locate the former members of IPW Team 94, on which I had also served. They included Dick Schifter, Morris Parloff, Werner Barth (who passed away in 2001 but is survived by his wife Jo), and also Adolf Rothschild, whom I did not locate until 2003 in a retirement home in Colorado.

My investigative skills failed me entirely, however, in finding surviving members of MII Team 499G, on which I served last of all in 1945. I have not been able to locate Charles Marshall, Rudy Kaufman, Kurt Lowenthal and Clifford Landwer.

Not on any of those teams but nevertheless affiliated with T Force of the 12th Army Group and important to this narrative, are Ozzie Backus, whose widow I was able to reach in Kansas, and Benno Selcke in Alabama.

One other person has been a major contributor to this work, namely, my marvelous wife for more than fifty-five years, Donna Riess Abt. She maintained the appropriate environment which enabled me to spend so many hours in front of a computer monitor. And at the end of the effort, she became the expert proofreader I could never be.

With gratitude to all those above,
Karl W. Abt

A Few Who Made a Difference

1

Arrival in France

On August 30, 1944, seven teams of the Military Intelligence Service disembarked on Utah Beach in Normandy. It was D-Day plus eighty-five. No newsreel photographers were present to record the event, nor would any Hollywood movies be made years later to commemorate it. The teams were made up of heroes of another sort than those who had stormed the beach on June 6. Their mission lay ahead of them in Germany, not in France. They needed to reach that destination intact.

Nor did the beach resemble at all what has been shown on newsreels or in the war movies. There were no longer any damaged or destroyed tanks and Jeeps. No concrete or steel tank obstacles placed there by the Germans before the invasion were to be found. And in the ocean surf, there were no shelled or disabled LSTs or LCIs that had carried the tanks and personnel to Normandy.

Instead, there were endless rows of crates and cartons and boxes on pallets, stretching as far as one's eye could see. It was the largest warehouse your writer had ever seen. No, it was the world's largest warehouse, and its roof was the sky. But tethered to the goods were long cables reaching up to barrage balloons three or four hundred feet high in the air. They had been placed there to discourage German fighter planes from strafing or shelling all that merchandise.

And why was all that merchandise out on a former combat beach instead of on docks and in warehouses in harbors? The answer was a simple one. The U.S. Air Corps had destroyed all the ports in France, as well as those in Belgium and the Netherlands to the north. The ports in Cherbourg and Le Havre were not able to support the Allied military operations in Normandy and on from there into France. That problem would plague the Allied efforts into the next year, when the port facilities in Antwerp, Belgium had been rebuilt.

Each team's two commissioned and four non-commissioned officers along with their two Jeeps and trailers had boarded a Liberty ship at the English port of Southampton on August 26, 1944. The ship crossed the English Channel two days later and put down its anchor in a French harbor near Bayeux. The next day, the teams transferred to a barge, which had to wait for the tide to change. Each team spent the night trying to rest in its vehicles and finally disembarked the next morning, August 30, near Valognes. It then drove a short distance to a Communications Zone tent city, where it waited for six days.

All the personnel took it easy in the tents. They caught up on their sleep and meals. Mail was received again from the highly efficient Army Postal Service, and there were opportunities to answer and mail letters. Some troops just enjoyed walking through the surrounding Normandy countryside. They knew that action lay just a few days ahead, for General George Patton's armor had broken through the eastern edge of the beachhead at Falaise, just south of Caen on August 22 and raced 125 miles to Paris in only three days. The retreating German Army fell back just as quickly, leaving tons of equipment behind.

The Military Intelligence personnel on the seven teams had been trained early in 1944 at Camp Ritchie, Maryland, located in the mountains about twenty-five miles west of Baltimore. Each month a class of trained intelligence specialists was graduated, following a course that lasted eighteen weeks. The principal qualification for attending the Ritchie course for interrogators was to be fluent in the German language (or in Japanese, for those headed toward the Pacific War). In fact, teams had even been prepared for possible military operations in Scandinavia or in the Balkan countries.

The members of the seven teams graduated from the 16th Class at Ritchie, in April 1944. Three months later, after a voyage of nine days on the converted ocean liner *The Brazil,* they arrived in Glasgow, Scotland. From there, they rode by train to the small village of Broadway, in the Cotswold Hills of central England, south of Birmingham and Stratford-upon-Avon. That village was the headquarters for the U.S. Army's Military Intelligence Service.

Every U.S. division that embarked for France with its nearly 14,000 officers and men received three intelligence teams of six persons. One team was assigned to each of the division's three regiments. The regiments had 3,100 officers and men, organized in three battalions. The intelligence team was there to question all enemy prisoners taken, in order to learn about the enemy force facing the regiment. It could help the military efforts immensely to know whether or not the enemy unit was at full strength and what sort of weapons it had, how much artillery backup was available, how good or bad the morale of the unit was, and answers to other similar questions. Surprisingly, captured personnel often gave such information quite readily, possibly assuming that their cooperation would secure them more favorable treatment. Actually, captured persons were all treated alike, in accordance with the Geneva Convention our country had signed in 1927.

The seven teams, however, became a part of a Task Force whose mission lay ahead in German cities to be captured. The Task Force was built around the 526th Armored Infantry Battalion. In other words, seven teams were attached to a battalion-sized unit, whereas an infantry regiment of three battalions had only one team, as described above. The vast difference was due to the unit's mission. It was created not to capture enemy soldiers but to enter German cities and towns along with the infantry and armored divisions. Once inside the city limits, the teams were to fan out and take over all military and political headquarters. Documents were seized which might prove to be useful to the Army's future operations or which might shed light on the motives and policies of the German government. Enemy personnel of higher ranks were also to be taken, but experience proved that they seldom waited to be captured.

The Task Force reported to General Omar Bradley's 12th Army Group, consisting of the U.S. First, Third and Ninth Armies. Those three armies were made up of six armored divisions and eighteen infantry divisions, with a total of about 350 thousand men. Information obtained by the teams was sent to the appropriate army headquarters of the division taking the city and from there, to General Bradley's headquarters, which had been moved to Verdun, France, closer to the front.

Technically, the teams were Interrogation-Prisoner

of War Teams, abbreviated to IPW Teams. Practically, they were often called by number, such as Intelligence Team 97, or simply Team 97.

The six men on Team 97 were Lieutenants Robert Kriwer of rural Pennsylvania and Paul Seiden (now of Calabasas, California), plus non-commissioned officers Max Siesel of New York City, Jan Polivka of Berkeley, California, Walter Waller of Boca Raton, Florida and Henry Griesman of New York City. Most of these men had learned the German language while they were young boys in Europe. Two of them were refugees from Hitler's Germany and have some interesting escape stories which will be presented later in this narrative.

There were six other intelligence teams in the Task Force, each with the same complement of personnel. One that was often affiliated with Team 97 was Team 94. It was made up of Lieutenants Werner Barth of Salisbury, North Carolina and Morris Parloff (now of Bethesda, Maryland) plus non-commissioned officers Adolf Rothschild of Colorado, Richard Schifter of Bethesda, Maryland, Henry Schuster of Northbrook, Illinois and your writer of Rolling Meadows, Illinois. At the end of the combat phase of the war, Schuster and Abt were transferred to Team 97, which in turn sent Siesel and Waller to Team 94 in preparation for anticipated changes in team duties.

All Task Force personnel wore the small, five-sided insignia of the 12th Army Group sewn at the top of their left sleeve. It was a geometrical design in red, white and blue. A red one-inch square appeared on either side of their helmets, with a white letter "T" centered in it. Some German soldiers who had been captured thought that stood for terror troops!

About the Campaign in Normandy

Much has been written about the invasion of Normandy in June, 1944. For those not inclined to read history books, such as B.H. Liddell Hart's comprehensive *History of the Second World War*, there have also been films, of which the most prominent include *The Longest Day* in 1962, *Saving Private Ryan* in 1998 and *Band of Brothers* in 2001.

The twin objectives of opening a Western front in France were to relieve pressure on the Russian forces already fighting the German armies on the Eastern front and to hasten the defeat of those forces. The British and American Allies, having already fought the Germans in North Africa and Italy, had debated the choice for a new Western invasion front. Some British leaders had advocated a southern strike through the Balkan countries. Americans favored hitting the northern coast of France. That became the final choice.

On that northern coast, the Contentin Peninsula of Normandy east of the port of Cherbourg and stretching to Caen was selected. The German generals awaited an attack farther to the east, between Dieppe and Calais, where the English Channel was much narrower.

The Allies employed a number of deceptive measures to direct the Germans away from the Contentin Peninsula. Heavy air raids pounded the coast near Dieppe and Calais. The body of a dead Allied officer was placed on the beach, with false orders specifying that the invasion would occur there. In addition to those tricks, all Allied units used code names, both for the units they were communicating with and for operational orders. The overall invasion, for example, was named Operation Overlord. More about the use of code names later on.

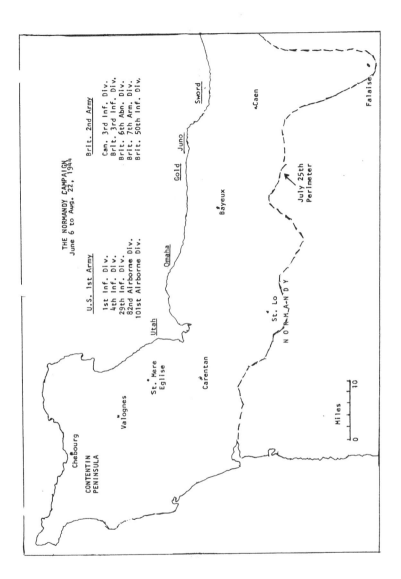

THE NORMANDY CAMPAIGN
June 6 to Aug. 22, 1944

U.S. 1st Army

1st Inf. Div.
4th Inf. Div.
29th Inf. Div.
82nd Airborne Div.
101st Airborne Div.

Brit. 2nd Army

Can. 3rd Inf. Div.
Brit. 3rd Inf. Div.
Brit. 6th Abn. Div.
Brit. 7th Arm. Div.
Brit. 50th Inf. Div.

CONTENTIN
PENINSULA

Cherbourg

Valognes

St. Mere
Eglise

Carentan

Utah

Omaha

Gold

Juno

Sword

Caen

Falaise

Bayeux

St. Lo

N O R M A N D Y

July 25th
Perimeter

Miles

0   10

When the date for the invasion, which would forever be known as D-Day, arrived, Allied forces were at British ports. Because the German air force had been swept from the skies, they were not aware of the troop movements. The chosen date was June 5, but Mother Nature disregarded Allied plans, as a fierce storm swept the English Channel. By June 6, it had not subsided completely, but the Allied Commander, General Dwight Eisenhower, gave the order to proceed anyway. The desired combination of tides for the ships and moonlight for the airborne troops who would be air-dropped behind the beaches would not recur for another month. As a result of landing from small vessels in a storm, many soldiers arrived at the beach seasick.

On D-Day, 5,000 Allied ships and 4,000 smaller landing craft brought seven Allied divisions to the Normandy coast, starting at 6:30 A.M. Earlier, paratroopers of three Allied airborne divisions had landed to disrupt bridges, railroads and airfields. Allied warships rained shells on German coastal fortifications, and 11,000 Allied aircraft controlled the skies.

Referring to the accompanying map, one can locate the Allied divisions mentioned and see the five beaches on which landings had occurred. The beach code names were Utah and Omaha for the American forces and Gold, Juno and Sword for the British and Canadian troops.

The American divisions encountered the heaviest enemy fire from the heights overlooking Omaha Beach. Nevertheless, they took their losses and scaled the heights. Then, they penetrated two miles into the peninsula, to begin several weeks of fighting in the hedgerows and towns that lay beyond.

The heaviest opposition was experienced by British troops at Caen. They had planned to take the city on the first day, only to encounter the sole German armored division. A second one arrived a day later, leading to a battle that was not won by the British until July 18.

Field Marshal Karl von Rundstedt was the German commander for the new Western front. He had placed General Erwin Rommel of North Africa fame in charge of defenses along the Channel. However, Rommel was on a trip to Germany on June 6. It fell to von Rundstedt and even Adolf Hitler himself to shift the German forces defending the Dieppe–to–Calais coastal area to attack the invading armies on the Contentin Peninsula. It is believed that Hitler had harbored a hunch all along that the peninsula would be the target of the invasion.

Within the first month, the Allies suffered 8,000 soldiers killed in action. Total troop strength grew to 1,000,000. Included in that total were thirty-one U.S. divisions, eleven from Britain, five Free French, three Canadian and one from Poland. By the end of July, the second month, the Allies had penetrated twenty miles into the peninsula.

The Allies' progress could also be measured by the following events:

June 27 Capture of Cherbourg
July 18 Capture of St. Lo
July 25 Canadian and U.S. 1st Army troops surround Falaise, capturing 60,000 Germans
August 6 General Patton's 3rd Army broke through the Allied-German perimeter South of Cherbourg and isolated the German forces in Brittany, to the south.

Other important events occurred far from Normandy. On July 20, a plot to kill Hitler with a bomb placed in a German conference room failed, though he was injured. Then, on August 15, the U.S. 7th Army plus Free French troops invaded southern France and advanced north to join the impending action in northern France.

The U.S. 7th Army and the French 1st Army landed near Cannes on the Mediterranean Sea and moved up the Rhone River Valley in Operation Anvil. They became the 6th Army Group and faced the Siegfried Line south of the 12th Army Group.

On August 22, the Allies broke through the Allied-German perimeter at Falaise and raced toward Paris, 125 miles to the east. The Normandy Campaign had ended, and the Campaign for Northern France had begun.

Back to the Narrative

The Task Force left the Communications Camp near Valognes for Paris on September 5. It included the 526th Armored Infantry Battalion with its 1,000 men and 75 armored half-track vehicles, the 31st Chemical Decontaminating Company as a special support unit and the seven Intelligence teams.

A cold rain accompanied the convoy as it passed through Caen in eastern Normandy, the scene of heavy fighting by British and Canadian troops until it fell on July 18. From there, it veered south about eighteen miles to Falaise. This small town had been captured in a combined action of the Canadian and First U.S. Armies. The armor of General Patton's Third Army broke through the German lines there on August 22 and reached Paris three days later.

The convoy quickly passed through Falaise and then resumed an easterly course to Paris, first following minor roads and then onto the main highway. Near the end of the day, it breezed through the suburb of Versailles and past its palace. By day's end, the Task Force was bivouacked in fields, and the teams sought refuge in a building assigned to the U.S. Intelligence Service. Paris had been liberated just ten days earlier. All realized that they were quickly catching up with the war, after landing in Normandy 85 days after the invasion.

The next day, it was still raining, so the troops were given free time. A few returned to Versailles to tour the palace. The guide who took them through explained that most of the precious furnishings had been stored in the basements, for protection during the war; one could see only beautiful, empty salons. The guide asked them to look at all the scratches on the wooden floors. Those, he said, were put there by the hobnailed boots the visiting German soldiers had worn. "You are more welcome because you have smooth soles on your boots!" he added.

Later on, there was sightseeing in Paris, followed by a late meeting at the quarters. As a trial run, the teams were to enter a city in eastern France.

The next morning, the convoy set out again, headed for Verdun, 145 miles to the east. American commanders did not like their units to spend too much time in Paris because the personnel would lose their combat readiness. Some large units, like infantry divisions were simply paraded through the city from one end to another!

The 28th Infantry Division, which had been founded as a National Guard division in Pennsylvania, was photographed marching in wide ranks down the Champs Elysées, with the Arc de Triomphe in the background. That photograph was placed on a U.S. commemorative postage stamp in 1945. A lieutenant was then quoted in the news, stating that the men in the front rank were from his platoon and that most of them were later killed when the 28th Division was mauled in December's Ardennes Battle (Battle of the Bulge). Their commander should have let them enjoy Paris while they were there.

As the convoy departed, the Parisians were still lining the streets, even though the city had seen its first American troops almost two weeks earlier. Their celebrations just would not end, it seemed. The lines of civilians pressed upon the convoys, from the sides of the streets, as closely as possible. Some of the faces in the crowd, young and old alike, became unforgettable, as they focused their glances on the troops and passing vehicles. What a moment that was!

About the Campaign for Northern France

With the breakthrough at Falaise on August 22, the Normandy campaign ended, to be followed by the Campaign for Northern France. That new campaign covered not only the advance of the Allies to the German border in France but also traced some divisions into Luxembourg and Belgium. It ended with the German counterattack in the Belgian Ardennes region on December 16.

The Allies raced from Falaise to Paris, a distance of 125 miles, in just three days, arriving on August 25. The German commanders, apparently not wanting that beautiful city to be destroyed by house-to-house fighting, declared it to be an open city and left with their troops. History buffs might try to obtain the 1966 videotape of the movie *Is Paris Burning?* to view the events of those days.

The victorious Allies entered with components of the Free French armies which had come back from their sanctuaries in England. Some of those events have already been described in the preceding narrative.

After liberating Paris on August 25, the Allies continued rapid advances into the remaining 200–odd miles to the German border. By September 5, they had reached that destination, encountering the fortified defenses the Germans had named the Siegfried Line. Many sections of that line faced its French counterpart, the Maginot Line. There the Allied advance was halted for more than psychological reasons, however. As explained in the narrative just ahead, the advancing forces had outrun necessary fuel and supplies.

The rapid advance of the Allies can also be measured by the dates on which cities in France, Luxembourg and Belgium were entered and liberated, as follows:

Verdun, France August 31, by U.S. forces
Luxembourg City September 12 by U.S. forces
Namur, Belgium September 4 by U.S. forces
Brussels, Belgium September 3 by British forces
Antwerp, Belgium September 4 by British forces

A September 19 landing of two Allied airborne divisions made to bridge the Rhine River at Arnhem, Holland, was not successful. The U.S. 82nd and the British 1st Airborne Divisions suffered heavy casualties. The equipment captured by the Germans was later used for diversionary and disruptive actions in the Ardennes Battle in late 1944.

In the autumn of 1944, heavy, ongoing fighting between U.S. and German forces also took place in the

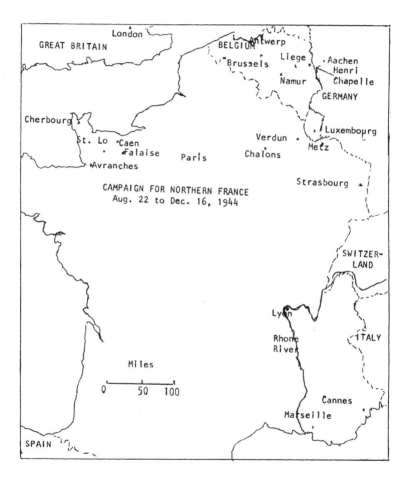

CAMPAIGN FOR NORTHERN FRANCE
Aug. 22 to Dec. 16, 1944

Huertgen Forest, located just within the German border southeast of Aachen.

The Ardennes, a wooded and hilly area in eastern Belgium and Luxembourg, is not a region experts would select for motorized military operations. Yet, German armies had already invaded through the Ardennes in 1914 and 1940. The U.S. forces occupied it quickly in September 1944, leaving small towns like Bastogne, Houffalize and St. Vith unscarred.

The Allied advances also resulted in a movement eastward for their military headquarters. The British moved into Brussels and SHAEF (Eisenhower's Supreme Headquarters-Allied Expeditionary Force) settled in Paris. General Bradley's 12th Army Group advanced to Verdun and also positioned a forward presence in Luxembourg. The U.S. 1st Army Headquarters located itself in the resort hotels of Spa, Belgium, deep in the Ardennes.

Back to the Narrative

Leaving Paris on September 7, the Task Force convoy moved on, through more cold rain. The city of Chalons, with a population of about 50,000, was the largest one encountered, two-thirds of the way to Verdun. The city was not damaged, and again, people lined the streets. They called out to the troops and waved their flags, which had been hidden away for more than four years.

Verdun was only half the size of Chalons, but had a long history as the center of battles, going back to Attila the Hun in 450 A.D. It is a fortified city on the banks of the Meuse River and only 50 miles from the Belgian border to the north which was the center of a costly, eleven–month long battle in 1916. Verdun fell rapidly, however, to the

Germans in 1940 and to Allied troops in late August 1944. A few days later, General Bradley would make it the headquarters city for the 12th Army Group.

The teams camped outside the city for five nights and were fairly comfortable. The rains ended the second day, and warm, sunny weather returned on the third day, making it possible for the troops to service the Jeeps , find clean clothing and spend time writing letters.

Every letter had to be censored by a designated officer. A soldier's letter could only identify his location as "somewhere in France," and could include no military information or data. The letters were mailed home postage-free. One simply wrote "Free" in the corner of the envelope where stamps are usually fastened, and the envelope had to have an A.P.O. return address.

The German troops had fled so quickly that they abandoned much equipment. A large German warehouse was discovered the second day in Verdun. It was very full but orderly. I found a pile of green German Army winter coats which had fur linings. I removed the lining from one and inserted it between the blankets in my own blanket roll, for added warmth during the coming winter. It did the trick!

The target city was another old, fortified one—Metz, about thirty-five miles to the east. It had a population of 100,000 and stood along the Moselle River. Metz was in the French province of Lorraine, which along with the adjoining province of Alsace had a mixed French and German population. The two were taken over by the Prussians after their victory in 1872 and then returned to France after its victory in 1918. The Germans recaptured those provinces in 1940, along with two similar ones in Belgium, namely, Eupen and Malmédy. It was their policy to incorporate them into greater Germany. Military personnel from those provinces who had been captured by the Germans were released to return to their homes, though the war continued to rage.

On September 12, after the five days in Verdun, the convoy moved to the small town of Neuberg, near Metz. The soldiers dug shallow trenches in the ground and slept in them. The Germans were shelling the area from the opposite side of the Moselle. Their favorite weapon was the touted 88-mm. gun. It was a versatile weapon, superior to many in the Allied arsenals. Since it could shoot both horizontal and vertical trajectories, it was used against personnel, vehicles and aircraft as well. Each soldier's pay had just gone up ten percent because he was in combat.

The shelling continued the next day. In fact, the following two nights were spent in an air raid shelter. A couple of abandoned German military offices were located in Neuberg and examined for papers that might prove to be useful. However, little of value was found.

On September 14, an intensive bombardment began. A nearby farmhouse had a colonnade of sorts around two or three sides of the adjacent farmyard, leading to the barn. A couple of men crouched behind each stone column in the colonnade, which were at the most three feet wide. A French lieutenant was one of them, a member of the free French, who had spent the past four years in England. Since he was a native of Metz, he had been designated to guide the Americans into the city.

The bombardment ended, but not before one shell had landed ten feet away from the lieutenant. The troops got up and started to move about again—but not the lieutenant. A couple of men carefully rolled him onto his back. He was dead, from a piece of shrapnel which had struck his jugular vein. Ironically, this man who had waited four years to see his home again was killed almost on its doorstep.

After that final shelling, the Task Force troops were pulled back from that immediate area. A camp was set up for the next five nights in a distant field with a grove of trees.

It rained for two more days. There was time to sleep and get some combat food. Some men carried out guard duty, in two-hour shifts. Best of all, two batches of mail arrived from the States.

During that time, hundreds of B-17 bombers from the Eighth Air Force in England pounded Metz in a daylight raid, to no avail. The combat divisions of General Hodge's First Army did not capture the city until November 25.

The Task Force mission to enter Metz was abandoned. The convoy departed again, heading for the capital city of Luxembourg on September 19, just seven days after it had been liberated from the German forces.

The thrust of Allied advances across France and Belgium was changing. The long supply line from the beaches could not furnish enough supplies, ammunition and gasoline needed to sustain the same pace of operations. Gasoline, for example, was being delivered in five-gallon canisters stowed in Army trucks and driven nearly 300 miles across France, in "Red Ball Express" convoys, while combat tanks and trucks waited idly for them. The Allied advance had reached the Siegfried Line which protected German borders—and there it had ended.

The Task Force mission in France moved ahead to Luxembourg, Belgium and Germany—four countries and five military campaigns in all—but no one could tell when it would resume or how or when it would end.

2

Roads to Luxembourg and Belgium

The convoy left for Luxembourg on September 19, headed for its capital city, also called Luxembourg, only a scant thirty miles to the north. No, what you've just read is not a mistake. Think of it as you do New York, New York.

The whole country has an area of only 998 square miles. One-fourth of its 300,000 people lived in the capital. It had been a duchy of The Netherlands for hundreds of years, until that association was terminated with the ascension of Queen Wilhelmina to the Dutch throne. The laws of Luxembourg did not permit a female ruler.

With such a small population, immigrants from that country are quite scarce in our own land. You will probably encounter only a few in your whole lifetime, but you will find them to be a very proud people.

Although T Force arrived one week after the initial liberation by American troops, it nevertheless encountered a terrific reception—loud and enthusiastic. And it did not end when the vehicles had all passed by, but it went on for days and days. Everyone had saved bottles of wine for the occasion, and there were warm greetings on the sidewalks and in restaurants. Many had studied the English language in public school and were eager to practice it with their new visitors.

The battalion camped on the outskirts, but the teams found shelter in a huge railroad administration building at the center of the city for the first three nights. Then they moved into hotels, which were vacant for the most part because of the war. For two days, all were free to walk about, photographing the old historic buildings and talking with the people on the sidewalks. They ate great meals at the restaurants, shopped for souvenirs, wrote letters home and even saw some recent movies from the States (as our homeland was called).

On the fourth day, the leaders found some duties for the teams. They listened and interpreted conversations of Army personnel with civilians who spoke German but no English, received more training in reviewing documents, and even had some practice on a rifle range. Most Intelligence personnel carried carbines or pistols, not the large M-1 rifle.

On the sixth day, Sgt. Ozzie Backus of Team 95 and I arranged to tour the caverns and catacombs located underneath the central part of the city. These were part of the strong fortress built hundreds of years earlier but still one of Europe's most formidable defenses.

All entrances to the caverns had been barricaded by the occupying German forces, in order to prevent their personnel from entering and becoming lost. The guide we had was a very knowledgeable high school lad recommended by a restaurant owner. Armed with flashlights and backup batteries, the three of us circumvented a barricade and roamed about the system for a couple of hours.

At frequent intervals, we found remnants of campfires and empty tins which had held food. The guide explained that many of his countrymen—both men and boys—had lived down there for extended periods of time in order to escape induction into the German military forces. In retrospect, Ozzie and I agreed that our visit down there had been a risky episode, but it ended without untoward results.

In the ensuing days, the teams had a variety of duties. For one thing, they gave lessons in the German language to the Task Force troops. There were also weapons instruction, hours spent servicing the Jeeps, talks and reports about German government and politics, practical exercises in photo interpretation, which we had all studied thoroughly at Camp Ritchie, and other activities.

But most of all, everyone had a lot of fun. There was more sightseeing, dates with local girls and lots of good meals. The favorite restaurant for many—Dichter's—had at least two marvelous banquets for their visitors. Years later, I stopped there as a tourist to tell the owner again how much we all had appreciated what he did. We had chances to send packages of souvenirs home, and some of us also attended Sunday services at the cathedral. They were in the local tongue, of course, which bears some similarity with the German we all knew.

By October 10, the Task Force leadership had received some instruction about its future role during the lull in the fighting. The teams were basically under the control of the Military Intelligence Service now in Paris, which was also making plans for them. They wanted to keep their interrogators busy, if at all possible.

The Task Force convoy left for Belgium, moving through Arlon, Belgium, and then in a northerly direction to Bastogne, Houffalize, St. Vith and Malmédy, on to Spa. It was an eighty-five-mile journey through the pretty hills and woods of the Ardennes Forest. The towns were as yet unscathed by the war, either from the German invasion of 1940 or from the Allies a month ago. That would all change in December.

Spa was a beautiful resort town of only a few hundred inhabitants but boasting health baths and several hotels. The U.S. forces were quick to establish headquarters there. The Task Force took accommodations as it had in Luxembourg, with the teams back in another hotel. The 4th Infantry Division, which had landed on D-Day, also had its headquarters there.

Our principal assignment was to prepare a listing and report on German officials, which took five days to complete from the various documents which had been gathered. When not working, we enjoyed the town's baths and attended a concert of the 4th Division Dance Band, a great USO show and some movies. Not a bad life for a few days.

On October 17, I drove a Jeep to the First Army Interrogation Center, just a few miles to the north near Verviers. Sergeant Ozzie Backus went with me. The personnel lived in a nearby village, while interrogating certain civilians at the Center. Some of them were being tested for work in the near future, while the fighting remained at a standstill.

The Center was near a large field in which all German prisoners taken by the combat divisions along the front of the First U.S. Army were held for one day. Along with the military prisoners were civilians who had been taken attempting to cross from the German side. First Army interrogators selected certain military prisoners for questioning. They also spoke with all the civilians who had been taken crossing through the German lines to the U.S. side, for agents were sometimes stashed among them. At the end of each day, the military prisoners were evacuated to camps in the rear areas and the civilians were released to continue their journeys, unless they had been found to be suspicious.

On October 20th, Ozzie and I returned to Spa and rejoined our teams. The next day, the teams moved about ten miles to the west, to the small Ardennes town of Remouchamps. They were billeted in a chateau for three nights and then moved again to one of the Ardennes Forest hotels in the town, for an extended stay. They spent a number of hours classifying and filing reference cards from SHAEF (Supreme Headquarters-Allied Expeditionary Force, that is General Eisenhower's headquarters in Paris).

It was at this time that we saw the first V-1 rocket flying overhead, as people had been seeing in England during the entire summer. The rocket was an unmanned weapon which flew at an altitude of only a few hundred feet, emitting a loud, distinctive rumble as it went. The instant one heard that rumble stop, the rocket was falling straight down. It would then cause an explosion that could destroy a medium-sized building and kill all those around. Obviously, the V-1 was a terror weapon. Its principal target at this time was the port of Antwerp to the north, which the Allies were rebuilding. Some of the rockets proved to be defective, however, and could be expected to fall short of their intended goal in the nearby areas.

On October 26th, I was detached from my team and driven back to the First Army Interrogation Center. Apparently, I had passed my initial interviews there, for I stayed with them until March 3, 1945, when the advance into Germany was finally resumed again. That period of eighteen weeks did not prove to be a quiet time, however, for it included the Ardennes Battle (also called the Battle of the Bulge). The front lines retreated twenty-five to thirty miles, and the U.S. incurred the largest number of casualties of the war in the European ETO (Theater of Operations).

The First Army Interrogation Center, whose code name was the MIC (Master Interrogation Center), was thirty miles northeast of Remouchamps, near the small Belgian village of Henri Chapelle, just inside the border with Germany. Today, many Americans have become acquainted with the small village, for it is the site of a large American cemetery with graves of those who perished in the Ardennes Battle.

A Belgian farm family, the Habetses, kindly offered me a room in their home for my stay there. They lived in the village and left each morning to work in their fields, as is the custom in Europe. In those days, they still used horses, and the occupying German Army had "requisitioned" some of them, so things were not easy. On a visit to the Habetses years later, I found that they had switched to tractors.

The oldest son, Josef Habets, had been in the Belgian Army in 1940. However, he was released from prisoner-of-war status when his province of Eupen was once again made a part of greater Germany later in the same year.

The MIC was in some Belgian Army buildings in Henri Chapelle, along Highway 3, which ran all the way from Brussels on the west to Cologne, Germany, on the east. Closer than those two huge cities, however, were Liège, Belgium, on the west and Aachen, Germany, on the east, only 30 miles from each other and also large cities. The field where newly captured prisoners were held for one day was about a mile away, along a minor roadway, requiring continual driving between there and the MIC.

So, Team 97 was in place at Remouchamps, while Team 94 would soon move from there to an assignment near Aachen, and I was in Henri Chapelle. Eighteen weeks lay ahead before the advance into Germany would resume. No one realized how eventful those weeks would be. Besides that, the Belgian winter lay just ahead.

3
Belgium in the Fall

With headquarters in Remouchamps, the six men on Team 97 moved around weekly, sometimes even daily, from one military unit to another. They interrogated captured prisoners (even before they got to the MIC) and interpreted German documents that had also been taken. They worked with combat units as well as with the CIC (Counter Intelligence Corps), whose principal mission was to detect and combat enemy intelligence personnel.

The team operated between the Liège area and Aachen, often in small places found only on the most detailed maps. Of course, they encountered all sorts of problems and situations. Henry Griesman, for example, was wounded on October 24 and sent to an Army hospital in Verviers. When released, he was sent to an infantry replacement depot! Fortunately, the team officers rescued him from there, and he rejoined the others on November 5.

Griesman has recorded multiple incidents of V-1 rockets crashing in the Liège area during November and December, after his return from the hospital. Some were intended for the Antwerp area but fell short of there, while others were clearly intended for Liège. Either way, the damage and injuries were often significant.

On November 22, seventy V-1 rockets hit around

Liège, killing sixty babies. The assault continued most of the week thereafter. A general hospital was hit, killing thirty patients. The city was then placed off limits to our troops.

On Team 94, with your writer attached to the MIC, the remaining five members went to the area already occupied east of Aachen and carried out duties similar to those described for Team 97. Of course, they were working in areas that were 100 percent German, where the U.S. Army was an occupying power. That required not only total use of the German language but also special skills and discretion in diplomacy, human relations and security.

Henry Schuster had an experience similar to that of Henry Griesman, of Team 97. He was not injured but contracted frostbite in both legs and was admitted to an Army hospital. When healed, he was sent to an infantry replacement depot (just as Henry Griesman had been). Lieutenant Barth rescued him from there, so that he returned to the team. Schuster was eternally grateful to the lieutenant for that!

I was released from my team, of course, to go to the Master (that is, the First Army) Interrogation Center near Henri Chapelle on October 26, until U.S. troops again advanced into Germany. That would not be for eighteen weeks, until the beginning of March. From time to time, I received a day off there and could visit my teammates. They also stopped by sometimes to see me and learn what the MIC was doing.

Each day, the MIC picked out prisoners captured by the divisions on the line held by the First Army from a large compound where they were held for one day before evacuation to safety in the rear areas. The daily population of the compound could vary from a few dozen a day to hundreds.

The very first day, I carried out two interrogations. Because the interrogation process has already been mentioned several times, it is now appropriate to include an abridged version of a rather long interrogation report. Though originally classified Confidential, that designation is no longer applicable.

The case involves a German soldier who was taken behind U.S. lines, in civilian clothing. Of course, this created suspicion that he might be a German agent. Hence, this interrogation.

Subject: Luckas, Johann, PW #31G980421

1. Subject, a German national, was arrested by the 301st CIC Detachment on 15 February 1945. He is charged with being a German soldier who deserted his regiment in Normandy and hid with a girl in northern France. Interrogation confirmed his status as an escaped prisoner of war, not a deserter who was hidden in France as a civilian. The circumstances of his escape revealed nothing of counter-intelligence interest concerning escape routes or contact people.

2. BACKGROUND. Subject was born on 11 December 1915 in Gau Algesheim near Bingen on the Rhine. He finished school in 1929 and then attended an agricultural school for the next two winters. Otherwise, he worked on his father's farm. He was drafted in November 1937. He has no political background and was not a member of the National Sozialistische Arbeiter Partei or the Hitler Jugend.

3. MILITARY CAREER. Subject, when drafted in No-

vember 1937, was assigned to the 87th Infantry Regiment of the 36th Infantry Division in Mainz He received basic infantry and cavalry training and became a corporal upon its completion. His regiment invaded Luxembourg on 10 May 1940, took part in the French blitz and remained with the occupying force in the vicinity of Paris. Subject became a sergeant on 1 June 1940. He claims his lack of appropriate political enthusiasm for the Nazi regime made him unsuitable for further promotions. In January 1941, he applied for assignment to a cavalry school in Mainz, where he remained as an instructor for the next twenty-one months.

4. In September 1942, all non-coms were ordered to combat units. Subject was assigned to a horse-drawn supply column of the 326th Infantry Division. He took part in the occupation of Vichy France. The unit was sent to Montreuil and remained there until 23 July 1944, when the division was committed in Normandy. It was virtually annihilated in less than a week.

5. DESERTION. He found himself a straggler on or about 2 August 1944 and subsequently joined another straggler, Anton Burkhardt. (They wandered about for a number of days but were never apprehended by the German military police. Luckas attributed that to their continual neat appearance.) Their wandering took them into Belgium, then Holland and then Germany. He stated that his intentions were to go home and await the end of the war, which his experiences in Normandy indicated to be only a number of days.

6. On or about 20 August 1944, they walked to the house of Miss Tina Gilles, a divorcée living in Raeren near Eupen, Belgium, by the German border. They were offered food, then washed and slept for about twenty-four hours. Since they had missed continuing with the trans-

port company that had taken them to Raeren, they decided to accept the invitation to stay a few more days and rest where they were. Luckas believed that the war was nearly over, so he thought it was just as well to let the lines cross past him. From that time on he wore civilian clothes over his uniform. The clothes had belonged to a former boarder at the house. He also destroyed his service record, which all German soldiers were accustomed to carry.

7. CAPTURE. Luckas and Burkhardt never left the Gilles house. There was a two-week long period in September when two occupying American soldiers were billeted there. Luckas described their soldier patches, which must have been from the 3rd Armored Division. He and Burkhardt gave them their weapons as souvenirs and believes the Americans must have known that they were deserters but did not turn them in. Neither did Luckas register with the U.S. military government, which he said he did not know was required.

8. In November 1944, just before an American attack, deserters were rounded up by the American authorities and evacuated as POWs. An Army chaplain who was billeted with Miss Gilles' sister and another officer took Luckas and Burkhardt to a POW cage, from where they went to the MIC enclosure.

9. CAPTIVITY. The two were shipped from there to a camp near Compiègne, France, north of Paris. There, the German officer in charge told all POWs in civilian clothes to volunteer for transfer to "better camp." They did so, and wound up in a camp run by the Free French in nearby Beauvais, where they found that conditions were unspeakably bad. They realized that the German officer who had sent them there had done so because he thought they were probably deserters.

10. ESCAPE. Security at the camp was also very poor. After several weeks, Luckas and Burkhardt escaped over a wall at night, along with two others. Separating from the others, Luckas and Burkhardt hid on a freight train headed north and left it near Liège. Luckas stated that his objective was to get to a camp in Belgium, where all POW camps were run by Americans, instead of by resistance organizations like the Free French.

11. ARREST. While they were eating some apples they had purchased from a farmer, a Belgian gendarme came by. When he spoke with them, they answered in French that they were German soldiers. Surprised at their frankness, he took them to gendarme station in nearby Ligney. They showed the PW cards they had been issued at the POW camp in Compiègne, but the Belgians could not read or understand them. Nevertheless, they turned the two prisoners over to the Americans.

12. REMARKS. Luckas makes an intelligent impression. The fact that the two soldiers billeted at the Gilles house probably knew the identity of him and Burkhardt without taking action arouses suspicion. However, inasmuch as the situation in which Luckas and Burkhardt found themselves was not unique, the soldiers may have taken it for granted that they were properly registered. It is very likely that Luckas' plans, always indefinite and changeable, were not to seek an American POW camp but to go to Raeren again and hide there. However, his frankness and passiveness immediately upon apprehension and the fact that he never destroyed his PW card would not indicate this. He can be considered a true POW now, as in November. No connections with the German Intelligence Service or information of counter-intelligence interest were uncovered.

—Tec 3 Karl W. Abt

31

Following this interrogation, Luckas was, in fact, sent to one of our POW camps in the rear areas. His interrogation did not reveal any significant amount of tactical information about the German forces facing ours. However, it did indicate that he was a true POW and not an enemy agent behind our lines. Identifying such agents was one of the primary functions of the MIC.

Besides conducting interrogations and writing the reports of them, I made a number of trips to Verdun, France, headquarters of the 12th Army Group, and to Luxembourg city, where its forward headquarters were located, in order to take prisoners there from the MIC who needed further interrogation or disposition. Usually accompanying me on these trips by Jeep was Sergeant Charles Herndon, who was also loaned to the MIC from an MII team, that is, a Military Intelligence Interpretation team. Those teams became increasingly important in coordinating matters with our Military Government people. In addition, most of their personnel spoke French, which was necessary in both France and Belgium.

Charlie, it turned out, belonged to the same college fraternity as I did. He had been attending Washington and Lee University, and I was halfway through at Northwestern University. As the miles sped by, we relieved the boredom by singing fraternity and college songs. A couple of the prisoners we transported said that we were the happiest Americans they had seen!

On the return trip to Henri Chapelle, we usually stayed overnight at Arlon, south of Bastogne. There each of us had friends he had met in Luxembourg city. Mine was the Muller family, where I was treated almost as a son, though my main interest was in their oldest daughter, Denise!

Delivering prisoners for further interrogation and possible imprisonment was not a cheerful task, but one of the trips was entirely different. On December 4, we took a member of royalty, a Baron, to be exact, back to his home in Luxembourg. He had been one of the civilians who had crossed the lines and then been interrogated at the MIC.

Upon arrival in the Luxembourg area, he directed us to his home, which was a country chateau on the outskirts. Of course, his return was a complete surprise, and his family rushed out of the building after he knocked. It was a grand reunion. He invited us to come in, but we refused, with thanks, because we did not want to interfere with the happy occasion. There were too few of them during this war.

The MIC kept a few trustee prisoners within its confines. One was Michael Jovy, a German still in his 20s, who had deserted, bringing his company's machine gun with him. It was known from SHAEF records that he had been a member of a resistance movement in Cologne. The movement was not a strong one, as might be guessed, but nevertheless it existed. The U.S. Military Government people planned to appoint him the temporary mayor of a German town, once the advance into Germany was resumed.

Another trustee was Anton Korn, a very professional top sergeant in the German Army and a more mature person than Jovy. He had no use for the Nazi officials who ran his country and evinced a desire for the war to end. The Counter Intelligence people wanted him to return within the German lines and act as a U.S. agent, gathering data about the forces which would be encountered when advancing into Germany. He was taken to a forward post in the U.S. lines and sent back, with instructions to contact the CIC people, once Cologne had been reached. And, such a meeting did occur. Admittedly, such arrangements were not foolproof.

One day before winter, a most unusual event took place at the prisoner-of-war-enclosure. A V-1 rocket, probably destined for Antwerp but a faulty one, stopped a few hundred feet in the air just above the enclosure. The roar of the engine ceased, and the rocket fell straight down. Everyone hit the ground and covered his head.

The rocket exploded into the soft dirt, digging a crater about a dozen feet deep and twenty-five feet across. As the explosion ended, prisoners began to stand up one by one and look about. Unbelievably, no injured persons could be found. The explosion was heard at the MIC a mile away, so some interrogators immediately drove there.

They decided that it would be a good time to conduct interrogations about the event, so a number of prisoners were taken to the MIC. Not only were they surprised by what had happened, but they were also extremely disheartened that a super weapon that they believed could win the war had done so little damage!

In late November and December, interrogations at the MIC revealed that a military buildup of troops and tanks was occurring behind the German lines. Henry Griesman recalls that Team 97 also obtained similar information in interrogations. Reports of these interrogations were received by General Dickson, the G-2 (that is, the chief intelligence officer) of the First Army. However, disbelief was registered by General Hodges, commander of the First Army, and General Bradley, who commanded the 12th Army Group, that any significant military operation was being planned. Only a few days later they both had great reason to regret the positions they had taken.

4

The Winter Ardennes Battle

About the Ardennes Campaign

The battle began on December 16, 1944 as the German infantry and tanks attacked along eighty miles of the Belgian-Luxembourg border regions. Twice before, in 1914 and in 1940, German armies had invaded there, in country that many military experts deemed to be too hilly and forested for normal military operations. However, it seemed to the attackers that the element of surprise would outweigh the disadvantages posed by the terrain.

Only four American infantry divisions stood in the path of the invading armies, each stretched thinly to cover its twenty-mile wide front. They were the 2nd Division to the north, with the 99th, the 106th and the 28th to the south, in that order. All were operating on the front of the 1st Army. They fought valiantly against the attackers, suffering thousands of casualties. The 106th Division alone had 7,000 men captured.

Against the defenders were twenty German divisions, seven of them armored divisions with 1,000 tanks. Though many were not at full strength but had been hastily assembled, they represented a massive force organized into four armies. They were led by Generals Dietrich, Manteuffel, Brandenberger and Model, all ap-

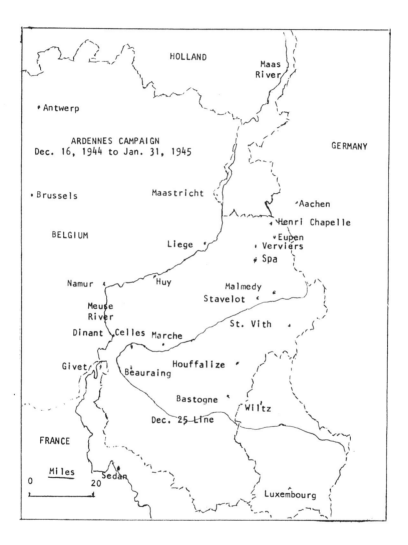

ARDENNES CAMPAIGN
Dec. 16, 1944 to Jan. 31, 1945

pointed by Adolf Hitler. The plan of attack was his, and he constantly directed military actions for them. Most German leaders were not in favor of the effort and reluctant to commit to it the last German reserves which would be ultimately required to defend their homeland. It was, in other words, a huge gamble intended to reach significant targets in Belgium and Holland.

If the generals did not favor Hitler's plan unanimously, the weather certainly did. Winter had arrived, with biting cold, snow and fog. Later, it was written that it was the worst winter for fifty years, making it the severest one of the century to date in Europe. Allied aircraft could not attack the enemy forces and armor for a full week, nor could critical supplies of ammunition and food be dropped.

Generals Model and Manteuffel were able to convince Hitler to change some of the tactical plans he had visualized. They suggested that the attack begin at 5:30 A.M. on December 16th, while darkness still prevailed and American troops were asleep. German artillery would only begin firing a couple of hours later. Rapidly, the attackers commandeered key bridges and intersections along the limited number of roads passing through the Ardennes Forest. When the German artillery began firing, it did not need to provide cover for their troops. Instead, it could concentrate on artillery positions, headquarters locations and ammunition dumps that the Germans had been able to identify.

Hitler planned another big surprise, coming from a battalion of troops led by the flamboyant Colonel Otto Skorzeny, who had rescued Mussolini in 1943. His battalion was made up of Germans who spoke English, wore garb which included some pieces of American uniform, and rode in American vehicles captured in the September airborne invasion of Holland. They penetrated the American lines quickly and caused much confusion by turning road signs about, cutting telephone lines and identifying nonexistent mine fields. Fully eighty percent of them were able to return safely. However, there are some interesting stories about a few who did not. Even those few teams which did fall into U.S. hands were able to create confusion and fear that many more existed and were roving behind the collapsing front line.

On December 17, SHAEF acknowledged the attack it had not believed would occur. General Simpson's 9th Army to the north of the new bulge was ordered to launch an attack on the north flank of the penetration. Similarly, General Patton's 3rd Army was to attack from the south. SHAEF also committed two divisions held in reserve to the action. One of them, the 101st Airborne Division, was to hold the road hub at Bastogne. General Patton also ordered one combat command of the 9th Armored Division into the town.

Within a week, the German armies had penetrated as far as sixty miles. They aimed for the Meuse River in Belgium, as well as for population centers like Liège, Antwerp, where port facilities were being repaired, and even Maastricht in Holland. And, of course, they needed to capture some smaller towns which were road hubs, like Bastogne and Stavelot.

The Army named the battle and the campaign the Ardennes Battle, but the American press rapidly called it the Battle of the Bulge. The points of deepest penetrations were in the direction of Beauraing and Givet by the German 5th Parachute Division, and to Celles and Dinant by the German 15th Armored Infantry Division. These towns were all situated just east of the Meuse River.

Including the 7,000 troops of the 106th Infantry Division who were captured, total casualties rose to 80,000, making it the most costly battle U.S. troops encountered in the European Theater of Operations. Most people do not realize that the losses exceeded those incurred in the invasion of Normandy. Visiting the large American cemeteries in Henri Chapelle and Luxembourg is a very sobering experience, showing the large percentage of the men lost who were killed.

Back to the Narrative

When the attack occurred, I was on the highway between Verviers and Malmédy and heard the artillery fire to the east. It did not seem real to me. The minute I was back at the MIC, I went to the room where a large situation map hung on one wall. I told Major Adams what I had heard, and he replied that it was real, for the German attack had begun, just as the interrogations had reported it would.

T Force's 526th Armored Infantry Battalion was drawn into the battle near Malmédy. Its tank destroyers blunted the German advance for a number of hours. Naturally, T Force troops also paid the price for that with their own casualties.

In Henri Chapelle, where Route 3, the principal road between Aachen and Liège, ran in front of the MIC, armored vehicles passed day and night for a week. They were comprised mainly of the 7th Armored Division, sent south by General Simpson. Whenever I was outside, I read the bumper markings on the vehicles until at last I knew the medical battalion was passing by. I stopped one of the passing Jeeps to ask about my second cousin, who was a doctor with that unit. Unfortunately, I learned that he had been evacuated only a few days earlier because of illness. So I never got to see him. However, the armor kept rolling and by the end of a week had pretty well torn up the surface of Route 3!

The German armies continued to initiate surprise in every conceivable way, and not just with Colonel Skorzeny's roving bands. Near Malmédy, they introduced additional terror by massacring 100 unarmed American prisoners of war in a wooded area. The German commander was later captured, tried and executed for his war crime.

The constant checking by military police and others to detect Skorzeny's men was not without its lighter and humorous side. One had to know the day's password in order to travel and also to give correct answers to other questions only Americans would know. (For example: the intricacies of baseball or the winner of the 1944 World Series or the identities of Hollywood stars.) Some MIS personnel, who had only arrived in our country in recent years, could not give correct answers and also spoke with heavy accents. They were therefore arrested along the highways and had to be rescued by their commanding officers!

The German penetration caused a general retreat of all headquarters in its path, at least to the Meuse River on the west or even further. The 1st Army headquarters in Spa, Belgium, left so quickly for Liège that it could not even assemble all its equipment. Consequently, several large resort hotels in Spa containing military records and documents, were hastily burned to the ground.

T Force also retreated to a couple of small towns east of Liège, after its battle at Malmédy.

After December 20, Allied aircraft once again ruled

the skies, and there were also many indications that the German attack had been repelled. However, the MIC moved back to the Meuse River on December 30. It occupied a high, prominent citadel overlooking the river at Huy, a structure built during the Napoleon years. It was large enough to accommodate the prisoners, too, who formerly had spent one day in the outdoor enclosure near Henri Chapelle. It was also closer to the military actions from which most of the 1st Army's prisoners were coming. As the German front continued to collapse, several thousand a day were coming to it.

The last day of 1944 was one of the most memorable ones in the entire war for me. I said goodbye to the Habets family, who had given me a room in their home in Henri Chapelle for so many weeks. It was to be thirty years before I saw them again!

On the drive to the Huy citadel with Major Adams, we stopped for several hours at a hospital in Liège. There we attended the trial of one of Colonel Skorzeny's men. He had been taken while driving in a captured American Jeep and wearing an American uniform. The trial was a general court-martial, before six high-ranking American officers.

During a recess, I had a chance to speak with the prisoner. He had been a ballet dancer with the Berlin Ballet and had learned English while touring the world. His commander knew that he had that ability, so had volunteered him for service with Colonel Skorzeny. He claimed that he did not go willingly but had no choice.

The tribunal found him to be guilty of spying, not because he was riding in a captured vehicle but because he was wearing a U.S. uniform. He was executed a few days later. To me that incident has always represented the tragedy and waste that war can bring into human lives.

Henry Griesman tells about the experiences of Team 97 during the attack. For several nights, while German bands roved the front and while their paratroopers were also being dropped behind U.S. lines, the interrogators carried out guard duty during the night. They camped in the woods despite the winter conditions. After that, they assisted the CIC at the 84th Division by carrying out patrols and road blocks near Marche, still looking for Skorzeny's raiders. It was February before they returned to the T Force.

At the MIC in the Citadel in Huy, I continued to conduct necessary interrogations and write interrogation reports, as more and more German prisoners came through. It was even necessary to conduct some grilling of wounded prisoners at a nearby evacuation hospital. There were also numerous trips to the 1st Army in Liège and one final trip to Verdun, followed by a visit in Arlon. Upon my return to Huy, I drove through both Bastogne and Houffalize and saw the ruins the attack had brought to them. Surprisingly, General Eisenhower was also on the road that day, and I saluted the General from the controls of my Jeep!

A pleasant change was the chance to see two USO shows in Namur at the end of January. One included the famous movie star Marlene Dietrich, and the other one, Mickey Rooney! What a treat for all us troops to see and hear. Other welcome changes were the Sunday morning services at the Citadel which were conducted by an interrogator, Howard Irwin, who had status as a lay preacher.

Near the end of my service with the MIC, I carried out an interrogation which I would like to summarize here. It was conducted according to the Camp Ritchie method. Only two persons were to be in the room: the prisoner and the interrogator. Every attempt had to be made to maintain a low key of discussion. There were to be no remarks like "Ah hah!" which would lead the prisoner to believe he had just said something significant. For the same reason, no high-ranking officer was to be present, and as little as possible was written down until the interrogation was over. That made the process a great test of memory!

One other factor should be mentioned. If there is reason to believe that a prisoner is not telling the truth or is hiding some of it, the technique employed is to get him to repeat his story several times. If he is fabricating, he will eventually forget what he has said earlier and start to contradict himself. Then, he can be pressured to "come clean."

This interrogation is concerned with a Belgian national who had worked in Germany and who was apprehended when he crossed the front lines. It was well known that German agents could mask as such persons. Therefore, interrogation was mandated. The interrogation was originally classified Confidential.

Subject: Thelen, Wilhelm, Prisoner # not known

1. Subject, a Belgian national, was arrested by the CIC after being apprehended by the 39th Infantry Regiment when he tried to cross the front between Gemuend and Hohenfried, Germany.

2. BACKGROUND. Subject was born on 21 April 1911 in Raeren, Belgium, near Eupen. He completed grammar school and an apprenticeship. After that, he had a succession of jobs, including working for his father, who was a building contractor. He was married in 1932

and had three children. The family lived at 65 Hauptstrasse in Raeren.

3. WORK IN GERMANY. In 1939, he accepted a job as a truck driver for Ganser Transport Co. in Aachen. He drove chocolate and beer made in Aachen throughout Germany and brought back a variety of goods from his destination. After the capture of France in 1940, he also drove there, bringing back food and sometimes even wounded German soldiers released from hospitals. In June 1941, he came under the direct control of the Dortmund office of the German Trucking Association. At the same time, he began using a vehicle of the Kluge Transport Co. of Berlin. His salary of 240 RM per month was sent to his wife, and he received 6 RM per day for expenses. When Kluge was destroyed by bombing, he received allowances from the Association.

For military purposes, he was classified as suitable for labor only because of a hernia operation in 1939. Therefore, he was not drafted into military service, and he was not a member of the Nazi Party.

He once drove food to the Dachau concentration camp but observed nothing of interest there. Other drivers told him that the camp always seemed quiet and empty when outsiders appeared. In 1943, he made a number of trips into Russia, as far as the Caucasus Mountains. In October of that year, he was wounded when his truck ran over a mine. Thirteen laborers he was transporting were killed.

4. WORK SINCE THE BREAKTHROUGH. During 1944, he mainly transported food for the people of Dortmund. However, on December 20, 600 vehicles gathered there to transport gasoline to the front in the Ardennes. Subject says that they left in convoys of 100,

but most were destroyed by Allied aircraft. He says that only twelve of his convoy made it through.

In January, all Dortmund drivers were ordered to report to Paderborn to begin training for the Volkssturm, that is, the People's Army. That action coupled with the fact that he had not seen his family since Raeren was occupied by the Americans in September convinced him to flee to Belgium. He forged a trip ticket and drove off.

He arrived in Gemuend with only cursory challenges, parked his vehicle in a deserted barn and then hid in a cellar with others for about three weeks. Only about forty German troops were there to defend the town. They were poorly trained and undisciplined, often looting the town for food.

5. CROSSING THE LINES. On February 20, the German lieutenant in charge notified the males that all able-bodied men who did not evacuate with his troops in the next twenty-four hours would be drafted into the Volkssturm. That evening, Subject left for the American lines with four others, walking along a cemetery and then wading a creek. After another hour, they were haled by an American sentry. They waved white handkerchiefs and shouted "Zivilist" (civilian). He walked with them for about five minutes to a house in Hohhenfried, where they were interrogated briefly by a lieutenant of the U.S. 39th Infantry Regiment. The men were then walked farther back for about fifteen minutes to another command post, where they were again interrogated. Subject gave the interrogator the location of the German command post in Gemuend. He and his four companions were then permitted to sleep until late the next morning. They were then taken farther back for more interrogation to obtain target information. Subject gave the location of a gasoline dump and told about destroyed fuel plants. They were then

taken to the Red Cross in Monschau, where Subject's four companions remained, but he was brought to the MIC.

6. REMARKS. Subject has traveled a great deal, but does not appear to be overly intelligent. He has been cooperative and given much tactical information but has had much difficulty with dates, times and the chronology of events.

He has no political background and twice experienced difficulties in Germany with his minor outspoken and anti-Nazi opinions. His desire to escape from Germany to avoid conscription is not completely convincing. It is therefore recommended that he be turned over to the Belgian authorities for internment until such time that his home in Raeren is far enough behind the front to insure maximum security to our troops.

—Tec 3 Karl W. Abt

Wilhelm Thelen also gave a wealth of data about life in the major Ruhr Valley city of Dortmund in February 1945. The government had declared it to be a "tote Stadt," that is, a dead city, following an air raid in November. That meant that it would no longer be rebuilt during the duration of the war. Its population of 550,000 had fled, leaving only about 15,000 behind, who lived in barracks on the outskirts. Only minor activity was carried on in its destroyed factories and mines.

Main streets had been cleared, but going was rough. Rail transport had also been destroyed, and there was no longer a municipal transportation system.

Food trickled in from the surrounding countryside by truck and was assigned to retailers. Long lines had to be navigated to purchase it. Milk was available for children only, through use of ration stamps. Meat, however, was very hard to come by, even by use of ration stamps, and a black market existed for that commodity. Cigarettes and cognac were also available on the black market, for considerable sums of money.

Utility systems had all been destroyed. Water could only be obtained from fire hydrants and water wagons. Only one newspaper was published anymore, one theater was in operation, and most persons listened to British news broadcasts, despite a death penalty without trial for anyone caught doing so.

Order was well maintained by a much diminished police force which employed many old men. Staunch Nazis were also still numerous, and there were always troops around to lend authority. The Volkssturm troops were trained in four large barracks east of the city.

These statements are but a brief summary of what Wilhelm Thelen narrated, but from them it would now seem that he was not lacking in intelligence, as stated in the interrogation report!

By the time this interrogation occurred, the bulge in Allied lines had disappeared. Thousands and thousands of German troops had been killed or captured, and the 1,000 tanks committed to the battle had also been destroyed or captured. Like the Allies in September, the German forces had experienced extreme fuel shortages.

Besides those shortages, other factors contributed to the collapse of the German efforts. The German Army Group failed to provide the promised number of captured U.S. tanks and trucks. Instead, camouflaged German vehicles were substituted.

In addition, Hitler's overall objectives of seizing Brussels and driving the British forces from the continent again were far too ambitious for the number of men and vehicles planned. Another complication arose because commanders in the German 6th Tank Army had been brought into the planning phase too late. Beyond that, the offensive suffered from inadequate reinforcements of men and ammunition.

A German attack on Maastricht could not be mounted because of the need to use the troops on the Eastern Front. That made it possible to utilize the U.S. 9th Army to attack the northern flank of the bulge. Further, the Germans knew the Allies had over 5,000 bomber aircraft while they had less than 1,000 (though some of those proved to be newly developed jets). The Germans also suffered from having only one battalion of paratroopers available.

In February, the Allied lines once more stretched along the German border. The MIC left Huy and moved to Welkenraedt, a small town just west of the border, lying between Eupen and Aachen. T Force was re-assembling in the area around Vieux Waleffe, east of Liege. Team 94 came there from its assignment in the Aachen area, and Team 97 ended an assignment with the 75th Division.

Divisions were moving eastward, with plenty of gasoline, ammunition and supplies. Allied planes ruled the skies, and engineering companies were on the move with their bridge-building supplies. The next target was the Rhine River.

**Luxembourg City
Liberated 9/10/1944**

**Winter in the Ardennes
Walter Waller (right) with friends**

Karl W. Abt in Belgium, November 1944

The Habets family in Henri Chapelle, who offered me a room in their house

MIC Interrogators (left to right) Howard Irwin, Karl Heidemann, Karl W. Abt, Willie Joseph, John French

Spa, Belgium, 1st Army Forward HQ before and after the Ardennes Battle

Citadel of Huy, 1st Army Interrogation Center 1/1/1945 to 2/20/1945

Meuse River as seen to the south of the Citadel

Team 94 leaving from Vieux Waleffe, Belgium 3/1/1945

Karl W. Abt by German Mark III Tank in the Ardennes Battle

Henry Griesman (left) and friend at the Cologne Cathedral

Bombed center of Cologne 3/7/1945

Suburb of Bickendorf showing white surrender flags

Sabotaged Moselle River Bridge at Coblenz 3/18/1945

Deutsches Eck in peacetime, where Moselle and Rhine meet

Fort Ehrenbreitstein, across the Rhine from Coblenz, was HQ for the U.S. Army of Occupation after World War I.

Bad Neuenahr, south of Bonn, HQ of U.S. 15th Army of Occupation 1945

Team 94 in Herten in Ruhr Valley. (Left to right) Dick Schifter, Adolf Rothschild, Lieutenant Morris Parloff, Henry Schuster, Karl W. Abt. Lieutenant Werner Barth was absent.

Captain Benno Selcke of the
T Force

Teams leaving at the end of Ruhr Campaign at
Wuppertal's Monorail 5/4/1945

Team 97 at Kusil. Showing (left to right) Lieutenant Paul Seiden, Henry Schuster, Karl W. Abt, Jan Polivka. Lieutenant Robert Kriwer was absent.

Jan Polivka at HQ Co. Mess, 28th Division

French Displaced Laborers heading home from Germany

Released German soldiers returning to their homes

Sabotaged autobahn near Kaiserlautern

Ernie Pyle Memorial Railway Bridge by sabotaged bridge at Mannheim

Bunkers and entrenchments of the Siegfried Line near Zweibruecken

Henry Griesman on a road block near Landsthul

Karl W. Abt at bunker on the Siegfried Line near Zweibruecken

At a damaged U.S. medium tank on the autobahn

Lieutenant Kriwer inspecting damage to a German 105-mm, self-propelled gun

Karl W. Abt and Jan Polivka at the gun

Henry Griesman, Karl W. Abt, and Henry Schuster at the border near Pirmasens

Henry Griesman with Ozzie Backus, who visited for a weekend

Jan Polivka at the town fountain in Alzey

War damage in Saarlautern

Bombing damage at Zweibruecken

Getting road directions from a farmer near Saarlauten

The cathedral of Worms amid the bombed city center

The city wall of Worms

Sabotaged tower bridge at Worms

U.S. bridge over Rhine at Mainz

1945 postage stamp based on a photograph showing the 28th Division marching through liberated Paris. The Division occupied the Rheinfalz from 5/8/1945 to 7/10/1945

French troops take over the occupation on 7/10/1945

Bad Schwalbach near Wiesbaden, MIS HQ after V-E Day

5

Target Cities on the Rhine

On March 3, I rejoined my teammates at T Force in the Aachen suburb of Eschweiler. They had made the thirty-mile trip from the Liège area two days earlier. But, before I could rejoin them, there were two final duties to perform.

The first was to drive the German Sgt. Anton Korn to the Counter Intelligence Detachment of the First Division. That was located east of Aachen, at Stolberg. From there, he would re-enter the German lines to learn what military units the U.S. would be facing. He was then to rejoin U.S. forces in Cologne, with that information. As was previously indicated, he did so and then remained with us.

The kind of data that was needed about the opposing German forces was the same as what was always wanted from a captured prisoner. That was to know the identity of the divisions, whether or not they were at full strength (usually they were not) and what the morale of the troops was. To assist in evaluating what was learned, there was a wealth of data on the makeup of a standard German infantry division. Regarding personnel and weapon counts, for example, there should be 17,000 officers and enlisted men, seventy-four artillery pieces, fifty-seven anti-tank guns, and an assortment of heavy infantry weapons. Similar data for an armored division showed 194 tanks, thirty-five armored cars, and 175 artillery pieces and large guns. And an armored infantry division was supposed to have forty-nine armored cars and forty-nine tanks besides its artillery pieces and large guns.

A second chore was to retrieve Captain Benno Selcke of the T Force staff, whom I had taken to Dreiborn near Monschau. He had stayed with another officer, who was a friend, for a number of days to observe the front-line operations of the Ninth Division. Taking him to his destination had not been without its perils, but the second trip there was quite routine.

After that, I said my good-byes to the interrogators at the MIC. They were a great group. During the ensuing years, I was fortunate enough to see some of them once again, both by design and also by accidental meetings in airports and large cities.

About the Rhineland Campaign

With the front once again along the German border at the end of January, Hitler and the German generals knew full well they had not achieved their objectives in the Ardennes campaign. They had suffered casualties and captured troops in excess of 200,000 men and had exhausted all of their reserve forces and equipment not already sent east to battle the Russians.

Mistakenly, they also believed the Western Allies had completely exhausted themselves in the Ardennes. Instead, the Allies were ready to strike in overwhelming strength.

Arrayed farthest to the north, the British 21st Army Group under Field Marshal Montgomery was poised to

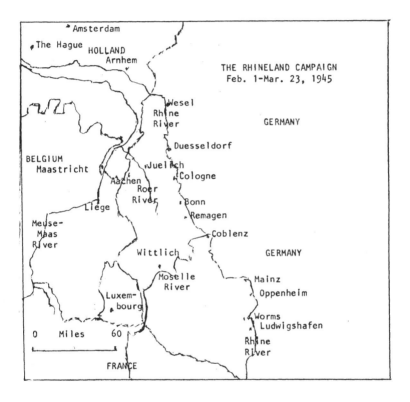

THE RHINELAND CAMPAIGN
Feb. 1-Mar. 23, 1945

75

advance toward Wesel and Duesseldorf on the Rhine River. It consisted of the 2nd British Army, the 1st Canadian Army and the 9th U.S. Army under General Simpson. The 9th Army had joined the 21st Army Group during the Ardennes Battle, much to the resentment of other American generals under Eisenhower.

South of those troops were the armies of the U.S. 12th Army Group under General Bradley. The 1st U.S. Army under General Hodges was positioned to take Cologne and Bonn on the Rhine River. The U.S. 3rd Army under General Patton was south of them. It was to take Coblenz, Mainz and Ludwigshafen, all on the west bank of the Rhine River.

South of Patton's forces was the 6th Army Group under General Devers, consisting of the 7th U.S. Army under General Patch and the 1st French Army. It had invaded southern France on August 15 and was focused on the Rhine River towns south of Ludwigshafen.

In the first week of February, U.S. 1st Army troops crossed the smaller Roer River, a tributary of the Meuse-Maas River just east of Aachen. By the first week of March, 1st Army's 3rd Armored Division entered Cologne. Other 1st Army troops took Bonn, south of there.

Just south of Bonn at Remagen, U.S. forces fortuitously found the only intact Rhine bridge, wired with explosives but not yet destroyed. They quickly dismantled the explosives. Though SHAEF would not yet approve the invasion of Germany east of the Rhine, 12th Army Group elements then proceeded to clear the west bank of the river.

The 3rd U.S. Army, which had taken Coblenz, where the Moselle merged with the Rhine, then crossed the Rhine almost unopposed at Oppenheim, south of Mainz.

Then, on March 23, General Montgomery's forces

carried out their planned Rhine crossing at Wesel. The 21st Army Group soldiers built bridges over the river after intense air and artillery bombardment, in an attack that also utilized two airborne divisions. Five days later, they had advanced twenty miles beyond the river. The Rhineland campaign was concluded.

Back to the Narrative

At Eschweiler, everyone was preparing for the forty-five mile trip to Cologne. The convoy set out in the afternoon on March 5th. It crossed the small Roer River, a tributary of the Meuse, which had been a battle line for a few days, as the military units advanced toward the Rhine.

The convoy stopped for the night at the small village of Stommeln. The team had acquired some folding cots, which could be used to convert any inside space to sleeping quarters for the night. That proved to be an excellent idea, at the beginning of a two-month period of continual movement. In Stommeln, the building used was actually a residence, but in future, there would be factories, schools, offices and tents as well.

The following day, March 6th, the convoy again left in the afternoon and arrived at the Cologne suburb of Bickendorf by dark, on the heels of the 3rd Armored Division. Again everyone settled into houses.

The city of Cologne was and is a large one, with a population of three quarters of a million persons in those days, but nearly one million today. However, in 1945, many of the inhabitants had fled to smaller towns in the countryside, in order to escape the heavy air raids, which had demolished much of the city.

Founded by Germanic tribes, it had been a Roman settlement in the first century, as had the smaller city of Aachen, through which the convoy had already passed. Both cities also figured prominently in the Holy Roman Empire during the Middle Ages. Situated on the west bank of the Rhine River, with suburbs across the river from it as well, Cologne is an important trade and manufacturing center today and has been since the Hanseatic League during the Middle Ages.

Say Cologne, and everyone automatically thinks of its famous twin-spired cathedral, which stands 525 feet high and was purposely left largely unscathed by World War II air raids. Started in the year 1248, the cathedral was not really finished until 1880. Remnants of the old Roman walls have been found near the cathedral in recent years and are visible in many other parts of the city.

The very next day, the seven teams with T Force fanned out across the city to search all the military and political office addresses which had been furnished by SHAEF. All the captured data received a preliminary review. Vital documents were dispatched to the G-2 of First Army, along with written reports. However, no military personnel were captured at the offices. They had not waited for our arrival.

On March 8, I accompanied the others on Team 94 on a most interesting assignment. It was a visit to the Ford Motor plant on the bank of the Rhine north of the city. Lo and behold, it had not been bombed and destroyed. However, it was searched, too, for key documents, but the principal find was nearly 1,500 foreign workers, many of them Polish but also some Russians and Italians. They pleaded to know what would happen to them.

All were assembled in the plant's yard. Then certain of the interrogators who knew Italian or Slavic languages, like Sergeant Jan Polivka, addressed them. They were told that the U.S. Army would feed them and eventually provide for the return to their homelands. For them the war was over, and that was the news they wanted to hear. It was a dramatic moment.

As for the team, it prepared a report for the G-2 of the First Army and then got ready to end its short visit and leave Cologne the following day. However, there is a sequel to what happened at the Ford Plant.

In November 1998, a commentator on *ABC World News* aired a segment on the use of foreign workers by Ford in Cologne. I immediately wrote to tell him what had occurred there on March 8th. Then I added that what was most surprising was not that foreign workers were there, but that the plant was not demolished or damaged, unlike many to be seen later in the cities of the Ruhr Valley. The commentator had alleged that there must have been collusion between Ford and the Nazis in regard to the use of foreign workers. I pointed out to him that such collusion must have extended to the U.S. air forces as well. When I worked for Ford as a financial analyst in the late 1950s and early 1960s, I asked many executives about that, but no one seemed to have an answer.

With the mission in Cologne completed, all headed south on March 9th to the next target. T Force was split temporarily, with some elements and teams heading for Bonn and the rest for Coblenz.

Bonn, also on the west bank of the Rhine and only fifteen miles south of Cologne, is a city of 300,000 persons today but had only 200,000 in 1945. It too was settled by the Romans and was famous for its university and for being the birthplace of composer Ludwig van Beethoven. It was to become the capital of the Federal Republic of Germany, until Germany was once more united in 1989.

There were military and political targets not only there but also in the suburb of Bad Godesberg.

The contingent headed for Coblenz, which was fifty-five miles south of Cologne on the west bank of the Rhine, opted to take the more secure secondary roads close to the Belgian border. It first skirted the Huertgen Forest, scene of a heavy infantry battle the previous fall, even before the Ardennes Battle. It then stayed overnight in two small towns in the scenic Eifel Mountains (also called the Snow Eifel). Then it stopped for four days at the tiny town of Nuerburg, situated due west of Coblenz.

Nuerburg was the site of a ten-kilometer race track built in the hills. It's called the Nuerburg Ring and is still in use today. Of course, there were no races to see then, but U.S. Army truck drivers were exercising their two-and-a-half ton trucks on its stretches. Simultaneously, Army artillery spotter planes were trying to use the straighter portions as landing strips, avoiding the trucks at all costs! All wondered how long the Army would tolerate the truck drivers' fun.

During the four days, everyone rested, ate, received mail and wrote letters. Some even enjoyed sponge baths in the warm sunshine! On March 15th, we moved through Mayen to Plaidt, a small northwest suburb of Coblenz. There another three days were spent idly, confirming the familiar Army game of "Hurry up and wait."

Coblenz is a city of more than 100,000 inhabitants today, though it was considerably smaller in 1945 and was also quite deserted because of air raids it had suffered. Location makes it unique, however, for it is at the confluence of the Moselle and Rhine Rivers, a spot known to Germans as the Deutsches Eck (the German corner).

The scenery is magnificent wherever one looks. The high bluffs on the east bank of the Rhine, which were still occupied by the German forces, feature massive Fort Ehrenbreitstein, which was the headquarters of the U.S. occupation force following World War I. The Moselle River itself flows in a northeasterly direction from France to the Rhine. The one hundred fifteen mile stretch from Trier, near the French border, to Coblenz is a miniature Rhine valley, with vineyards and beautiful small towns and castles every few miles and is well worth a day's drive today.

The three days of waiting were spent in an abandoned house, which was really quite comfortable. Someone was sure to return to it someday soon. The one drawback was that an artillery battery was positioned nearby, lobbing shells at the German Army across the Rhine, which could shorten one's sleep. The troops cooked their meals, washed clothes, cleaned weapons and wrote letters.

On March 18, we left at 0700 hours, driving the Jeeps to the Moselle River. Everyone crossed the river on foot and continued on to the main city area to the east. We were advancing with elements of the 87th Infantry Division, on the heels of their initial attack.

Fallen soldiers still lay on the ground along the way, sad to see, for most of us now had the feeling that the war was entering its closing days. Advancing into the city, we saw a lot of damaged and destroyed buildings. However, we again found some decent abandoned quarters in an apartment building.

The following day, our vehicles caught up, and the teams carried out the target raids. It was a busy day, as each team went from one location to another. In the main post office, I even walked away with a huge Swastika flag! That did not have to be sent in with the reports!

On the next day, March 20, Team 94 crossed to the

north bank of the Moselle again, in order to raid targets in the Metternich section of the city. We were met with success and even had a meal with the infantry unit positioned there. Just west of there, the Moselle vineyards were laid out to catch the sun's rays shining on the north bank of the river. There was little evidence of war in that beautiful region.

The following day, Team 94 raided more targets farther to the east. One was the home of a high ranking officer in the Brown Shirts (the *Sturm Abteilung* of the Nazi Party). Of course, he was nowhere to be found, but we decided to confiscate one of his highly decorated uniforms. On leaving his home, though, the team came under rifle fire from the nearby heights and speeded away in Jeeps as fast as possible. Fortunately, the German Army had lost or abandoned most of its heavier caliber weapons.

At 1100 hours the next morning, March 22, T Force left Coblenz. All the targets had been visited, reports were written and data was sent to the G-2 of the Third Army, headed by George Patton, of course. Again T Force was to be divided, for the final time, as it turned out.

The southern elements would proceed on to targets in Wiesbaden, Mainz and Frankfurt, in the valley of the Main River tributary of the Rhine. The rest were to head back north, into the First Army sector and enter the industrial cities along the Ruhr Valley tributary. Those who had gone to Bonn also went there.

At that time, I expressed a heavy preference to go on to the Ruhr Valley, where some of my father's relatives lived. That choice was respected, so I remained with my teammates on Team 94 to head for the Ruhr with them.

Under any circumstances, the war was winding down, and we could very well be facing the final operation. The Rhine River had been bridged, both by the fortuitous capture of the last standing bridge at Remagen, which the Germans had fitted for demolition, and also by the engineers in the Third and Ninth Armies. Armored and infantry divisions were pouring across the last natural barrier to the complete occupation of Germany. American morale could not have been greater, unless it was to hear that the war had finally ended.

6

Targets in the Ruhr Valley

The first leg of the trip from Coblenz was a short one. Leaving at 1100 hours, we traveled only to Plaidt. There we had a chance to clean up again after four days in a city which, for the time being, lacked customary water and utilities. Mail from home was also waiting for us.

On the following day, we left at 1800 hours for Cologne, traveling most of the way after dark. However, we took a more direct route instead of following the roads near the border. Upon arrival, we settled in the suburb of Bickendorf again. There I once more ran into Capt. Benno Selcke of T Force, a fellow resident of Illinois who now lives in Anniston, Alabama, and had a good chat with him.

We stayed one day, to prepare for the Ruhr Valley operations. It would be well to describe this region of Germany now. The Ruhr River flows from the east and empties into the Rhine at Duisburg. More than twenty-five cities are packed into its valley, one next to the other, and all participating in the variety of industries found there. On any map, the region is a solid urban mass.

On March 25th, which was Palm Sunday, T Force left the Cologne area and traveled thirty-five miles north to Moers, a smaller city of 40,000 inhabitants just west of

Duisburg and the Rhine River. There we found some vacant apartments which became our headquarters for the next fifteen days, while the teams conducted target raids in the western part of the Ruhr Valley. All of us knew that it was a religious holiday, for services had already been held the evening before departing.

While Team 94 and others began target raids in the western Ruhr cities, I drew headquarters duties for about three days. Someone had to keep track of the cities visited, type the team reports and organize the documents which had been confiscated. One of the evenings, after I was finished for the day, I even had the chance to attend an impromptu concert of the 84th Division Band. A real treat, since I had played in school and college concert bands for a number of years.

About the Campaign for Central Europe

The last campaign on the Western Front—the Campaign for Central Europe—began when the 21st Army Group crossed the Rhine River at Wesel on March 23. The map on Page 87 shows Wesel downstream (that is, north) of Duesseldorf. Just beyond Wesel, the river swings west to flow through Holland.

The 21st Army Group then split into two large segments in order to encircle the industrial Ruhr River Valley. Its 1st Canadian Army and 2nd British Army passed around the cities on the north side of the valley, as its 9th U.S. Army passed on the south side. In just a little more than two weeks, the segments met between Hamm and Paderborn. More than 300,000 German troops were encircled, but the fighting continued until nearly V-E Day on May 8.

Meanwhile, the other armies were racing east to meet the Russian armies. General Hodges' 1st U.S. Army headed through the state of Hesse to the large city of Kassel. General Patton's 3rd U.S. Army was south of them, heading for Leipzig. West of there, they linked up with the Russians on April 25 at Torgau on the Elbe River. Farthest to the south, the 6th Army Group stepped off from Strasbourg, headed for Stuttgart, Munich and Austria,

In the closing days of the conflict—in April and May—key events followed one another with seeming increasing rapidity. On April 12, President Roosevelt died, just weeks after his inauguration for an unprecedented fourth term.

On April 28, Premier Mussolini and his mistress, Claretta Petacci, were killed by Italian partisans at Lake Como, as a general uprising gripped the nation.

The death of national leaders was not yet over. On April 30, Adolf Hitler ordered his own execution and that of his one-day bride, the actress Eva Braun. He also ordered their bodies to be burned. Too late, he had come to the realization that he should have negotiated an end to the war before his country was completely pulled down and destroyed.

Three surrender dates occurred in rapid succession. The first one—April 29—occurred in Italy, where all fighting ceased three days later. On May 4, German generals in northwest Europe surrendered to Montgomery in Lueneburg. The third surrender on May 7 was at Reims, France, then Eisenhower's headquarters. It involved all German forces and was attended by American, British, French and Russian representatives. The next day, May 8, 1945, became V-E Day.

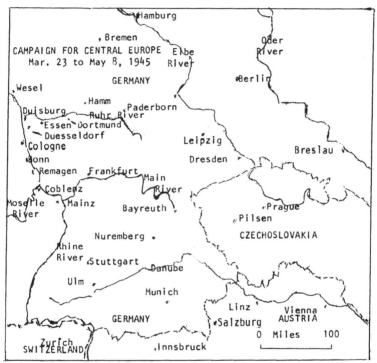

CAMPAIGN FOR CENTRAL EUROPE
Mar. 23 to May 8, 1945

Note: German-Polish border not shown

Back to the Narrative

On March 30th, interrogators from several of the teams had a different assignment. They conducted a survey of public opinion in Moers and sent it in a couple of days later. In all, they spoke with 103 residents, covering both sexes, all ages and many occupational groups. The report was four typewritten pages long, but it is condensed here, covering the five general areas of discussion.

A. Attitudes toward the American occupation: The population had listened to Allied radio broadcasts and spoken with German soldiers. They believed they would receive fair treatment and had already begun to see that. A few diehard Nazis still believed their party's propaganda that Americans would commit atrocities. Others had concerns about food supplies, curfews and travel restrictions.

B. Attitudes toward possible occupation by other powers: Little animosity was expressed if the forces were to be British, French, Belgian or Dutch. Some of the older persons had already experienced occupation following World War I. Most did not believe the horror stories that had been disseminated by the Nazis. Nevertheless, almost all did not expect fair treatment if the occupiers were Russian or Slav forces.

C. Estimation of political attitudes: Everyone asserted that he was solidly anti-Nazi now. In prior years, the Zentrum Party and Social Democrats had been strong in the area. However, it was quite clear that the majority had jumped onto the Nazi bandwagon.

D. Attitude toward war criminals and a possible Nazi underground: Most knew about some of the atrocities that had been committed and many had their own scores to settle with the Gestapo and Nazi Party officials. They believed, however, that their own countrymen would levy harsher punishment on war criminals than the Americans would. The possibility of an underground was largely discounted because no one wanted to lift a finger to aid a discredited gang of criminals.

E. The future of Germany: Older persons who had voted before 1933 expressed the opinions of their former parties on this topic. Because the Nazis had stifled independent thought, many intended to keep clear of politics. That included the young. There was an impression, however, that opposition to the Nazi regime was grounded mainly in the fact that it had lost the war.

Those who did express an opinion about the future of Germany were principally those who were older and who had other political affiliations before the Hitler years. Most interviewees do feel a guilt for Germany's treatment of the Jews and other conquered nations. They expect a long occupation and many expect conflict between Russia and the other Allied nations, though some expect world unity under the United Nations.

Most do not expect Germany to have an independent government in the foreseeable future. Younger persons were particularly confused by such a prospect, since they do not know what a democracy is. They did hope that they could choose their occupations but are resigned to whatever time brings them.

In all, it appeared that the interviewees believed their nation is made up of superior people who could deal successfully with the course to be taken in the future. One doctor stated that proper schooling along humane, democratic lines could completely change the country and eradicate the Nazi doctrines. And so the report ended.

Once that was completed, target raids resumed

again. Team 94 drove twenty miles to the south, to the larger city of Neuss, just west of Duesseldorf. We were there only one day. At night, we came under artillery fire and slept in a cellar. The next day we returned to Moers.

On April 6th, we drove twenty miles to the east, to the smaller city of Sterkrade. There, at the Ruhr Chemical Works, I served as an interpreter for the chemists who were being interviewed by Military Government personnel. In fact, all of us worked with MG for the next couple of days and enjoyed their meals much more than those we usually got!

A more permanent change occurred on April 9th, when we moved thirty miles east to Herten, a city also about the size of Moers but located on the north side of the Ruhr municipal complex. There, it was decided that another public opinion survey was in order, for use by MG in their future operations. The sample was only one third as large—thirty-five persons—and it was done with only five interrogators. Again, they covered the same five areas of discussion. The following are the differences that were noted from the survey in Moers.

A. Attitudes toward the American occupation: Interviewees are generally pleased with the American MG and the German officials that have been chosen to work with it. The food supply in the city is also good.

B. Attitudes toward the possible occupation by other powers: Many of the workers in Herten are coal miners, who had themselves exhibited some leftist tendencies before 1933. They do not feel much anxiety about the future role of Russia. They will welcome the end of the war. Some said that if temporary inconveniences and injustices occur, they realize that German occupations too were far from ideal, especially those by SS troops.

C. Estimation of political attitudes: Except for the large Catholic population which adhered to the Zentrum Party before 1933, most of the rest of the population was enthusiastic toward the Nazis and still fears to criticize them, probably because of their fear of free speech.

D. Attitude toward war criminals and a possible Nazi underground: There are no differences in this area of discussion from what was found in Moers.

E. The future of Germany: The main difference found in this area from what had been learned in Moers is that the older population, which includes many miners with leftist tendencies, express a hope for a liberal form of democratic government.

On April 12th, the teams drove south through Gelsenkirchen to Essen, where they settled in the suburb of Altendorf. Along the way, they stopped at the giant Krupp Steel Works, which had provided so much armament for the German forces. There was heavy damage, of course, but also evidence that rebuilding had occurred there more than once.

Target raids began the next morning and continued for two days. There were even some persons at the targets to interrogate. At the end of the second day, on April 14, I had one of the most personal and unusual experiences of the war. Not many soldiers could claim a similar experience.

My father, also named Karl Abt as were his father and grandfather, came from Kettwig, a small, pretty suburb about seven miles south of the center of Essen. It was situated north of a sharp bend in the Ruhr River and is hundreds of years old. I knew that at least three first cousins were living there who were the children of my father's sister, Emmy Abt Hayn.

Sgt. Jan Polivka of Team 97 volunteered to accompany me on a visit to see them, if possible. We took one of the team's Jeeps and left, after being warned that there was still rifle fire in the Kettwig area, originating from the hills across the Ruhr from the town. Of course, we promised to be cautious in our approach.

Upon arriving at the center of Kettwig, we were directed to the home of the mayor, called the Buergermeister by Germans, of course. He was at home and told us the exact street address of the Hayn family, which was on the Ruhrstrasse, along the river. I drove there with Jan, and got out to knock timidly on the front door of the large, two-story building we had found at the address.

A window was opened on the second floor, and a woman there called out, "*Was wollen Sie?*" I answered her, "*Ich bin Karl Abt von* Chicago!" The front door opened, and several people poured out. They were my cousins Gerda and Ilse, my cousin Helmut on crutches, their mother Emmy and several young children. Loud greetings were exchanged, and then Jan and I were invited inside.

We learned that the family had seen much, too much war. Gerda, the oldest, was married to a veterinarian who was practicing his occupation in the German Army, which still used horses. Ilse and her two young daughters were waiting for news of her husband, who was missing in Russia (it never came). Helmut was discharged from the German Army, after suffering severe frostbite in Russia. He lost both legs below the knee and was wearing artificial limbs and walking with crutches.

Throughout the visit, Jan and I felt no animosity whatsoever. When we left, I had to promise to return at least one more time.

The following day, four of the team conducted a survey of opinion in Essen, eliciting responses from a small group of fifty persons. Because the U.S. occupation had only lasted three days, some respondents were uncertain of their answers, so the survey was finished a week later. Most of the findings paralleled those in Moers and Herten. One difference was that Essen had had a large percentage of adherents to the Social Democratic Party who were now favoring "middle of the road" approaches in politics.

Regular education of school children had not taken place for over two years. However, most of the children had been evacuated elsewhere to escape the air raids. Many respondents believed that they, as well as the adults, were cured of Nazism.

At this point, mention should be made that Henry Schuster of Team 94 had grown up in Essen and began high school there. When the persecution of the Jewish population began in the late 1930s, with the smashing of windows in stores which had Jewish owners, Henry's family emigrated to the States. They settled on the south side of Chicago, where Henry completed his education at Hyde Park High School. A couple of years later, he was inducted into the service with other young men. His knowledge of the German language proved to be just what the Military Intelligence Service needed. Many other Jewish refugees found similar military careers, so the teams at T Force had an abundance of interrogators with that background.

Target raids continued in all the surrounding cities: Bottrop, Muehlheim, Oberhausen, Dortmund and so many others. The question has often been asked if anyone ever encountered evidence of atrocities in the Ruhr Valley. One comes to mind, which occurred during the first explorations of Essen. There, in the entrance to an underground subway, our team saw dozens of dead bodies, apparently all male. The Graves Registration personnel were notified. Upon asking passing civilians what had happened there, they responded that the men had all been killed in an air raid. A convenient explanation, it seemed.

On April 16, two days after my first visit to the relatives in Kettwig, I returned there for an afternoon. This time I brought along two items that had become valuable to the civilian population for bartering—coffee and cartons of cigarettes. Other essentials could be obtained with these, where transactions with money failed.

Again, there was a pleasant visit, which included a special treat. Helmut took me to the home of my great uncle, Otto Abt, and his sister, Friedchen Abt. Never married, they shared a small house. Otto was my father's favorite uncle. He and Friedchen came from a family of eleven siblings, none of whom had ever migrated and still lived in the Ruhr cities. And so, I enjoyed afternoon tea with them. It turned out to be the only time I ever saw them, for by the time my next trip to Germany occurred, they were no longer living.

Readers who may remember something about the Army's non-fraternization policy will question why these visits were permitted. Well, the policy was ignored more than observed. No one ever heard of anyone disciplined for fraternizing. Certainly, in this case which involved close relatives, no one criticized me.

On April 23, the teams returned to Herten, which proved to be the last town where we would see wartime duty. The Ruhr Valley operations had been successful. There was no more German resistance. Some divisions had already sped 125 miles east, to the banks of the Elbe River, where they met the Russian forces on April 25.

Despite all the apparent successes, there were still losses and failures which resulted in deaths. For instance, I learned later on that my college fraternity brother, Tom Cartmell, had been a pilot of one of three night fighters flying over the Danube River on April 26th. The entire flight was shot down by U.S. anti-aircraft fire, an incomprehensible action in view of the fact that the Germans had nothing in the sky anymore. Years later, I visited Tom's grave in an American cemetery in the French province of Lorraine.

After the surrender at Reims, France, on May 7, the European war was over at last. However, for the teams of the MIS, there was still much more to do.

7

V-E Day and Back
to the Rhineland

After the surrender agreement had been signed on May 7, the following day became V-E Day (for Victory—Europe). In all the Allied capitals, large cities and small towns, celebrations occurred to mark the end of a horrific war five years plus eight months long that had claimed tens of millions of lives. And on the anniversary dates years later, photos are still printed and film is run to remember the event. One of my favorites that is always seen shows the sailor in Times Square in New York City who lifts the nearest pretty girl in the crowd and plants a long kiss on her!

Germany was not nearly as boisterous on V-E Day, but nevertheless, a large sense of relief was evident, cautioned by concern about what the future would bring.

The teams had left Herten in the Ruhr in advance of V-E Day, on May 4 and proceeded to Bad Neuenahr, a pretty resort town west of the Rhine and south of Bonn. There some teams were released from T Force and attached to the 23rd Corps of the 15th Army of Occupation. In addition some personnel reassignments were carried out between the teams to prepare for some different duties, as follows:

Corporal Henry Schuster and I were assigned to

Team 97, which was already staffed with Lieutenant Robert Kriwer, Lieutenant Paul Seiden, Sergeant Jan Polivka and Corporal Henry Griesman; Sergeant Walter Waller and Sergeant Max Siesel left Team 97 to go to Team 94, which already had Lieutenant Werner Barth, Lieutenant Morris Parloff, Sergeant Richard Schifter and Sergeant Adolf Rothschild.

Team 97 left in the rain the next morning, driving along the Rhine to Bingen, then southwest through Bad Kreuznach to Idar-Oberstein. That town, known for its jewelry production, was a headquarters for the newly formed 23rd Corps. In that quiet setting, we spent the weekend which saw the signing of the surrender agreement at Reims, followed by V-E Day. Principal activities were to attend a church service, write some letters, rest and read. Nor should one leave out the bull sessions and a chance to see a movie! The radio broadcasts of the Armed Forces Network had featured speeches and patriotic music all day long. At 2400 hours (that is, at midnight), the war officially ended.

Idar-Oberstein is a scenic town located more or less in the center of the German province of Rhineland-Palatinate. That province of 7,600 square miles stretches from the Rhine to the western border of Germany, as does the larger province of North Rhine-Westphalia to its north. The main cities in the Palatinate are Coblenz on the north, Trier to the west and Mainz, Worms, Ludwigshafen and Speyer on the east along the Rhine. Near the southern end is Kaiserslautern, which was destined to become a major occupation center for the U.S. forces for years to come. G.I.s today call it K-Town!

On the lower west side of the Palatinate, the small Saarland province of 990 square miles borders France. It

97

Bad Neuenahr

0   16
Miles

Cobkenz

Moselle Rhine
River   River   Bad Schwalbach

Wiesbaden
Frankfurt
Bingen   Mainz

Bad Kreuznach

Alzey
Idar-Oberstein

Trier   Worms
LUXEM-
BOURG   RHINELAND-PALATINATE

Mannheim
Ludwigshafen
Kaiserslautern
Neustadt
Speyer

Homburg
Waldfischbach
Voelklingen   Zweibruecken
FRANCE   Saarbruecken
St. Ingbert   Pirmasens

Karlsruhe

98

was a part of France between the world wars, but was ceded to Germany in 1957, following an election.

After the weekend, Team 97 moved to Kaiserslautern and received luxurious quarters from the Military Government for the next five weeks in the home of a former high-ranking Nazi official. On a humorous note, his family continued to reside in the neighborhood, and one of the team members even became rather well acquainted with a pretty daughter!

However, there was work to be done, and it started soon enough on May 10. And what was it? Believe it or not, many more target raids. Apparently, Patton's Third Army had moved through the Palatinate so rapidly that many targets were never visited. And to whom did the team report its findings? To none other than the G-2 of the 28th Division, which occupied the province; the same division, of course, which is shown on a commemorative U.S. postage stamp marching through Paris, before suffering huge losses in the Ardennes Battle.

Included among the targets were the bunkers of Germany's Siegfried Line along the border with France. It faced the opposing French Maginot Line. However, the work did not start with the bunkers but instead at some nearby ammunition dumps and army barracks. In Germany, army barracks can be found in all sizable cities. They are often multi-storied and made of permanent materials, like apartment buildings.

On May 12, we drove twenty miles to the south, to some targets in Pirmasens, just north of the French border. The scenic highway skirted the western edge of a large state park called the Pfaelzer Wald. On the following day, we visited Homburg and Zweibruecken to the west of Pirmasens for three days of investigations. Near those cities, we investigated the bunkers along the

99

Siegfried Line, entering them very carefully in the event they were still booby-trapped. We found little documentation left behind but did get lots of photographs, not only of the bunkers but also of the fields of "dragon teeth" tank obstacles.

During that period, censorship regulations on letters were lifted. This meant that one could reveal exactly where he was, not just "somewhere in Germany." Likewise, one could relate where he had been in all the other countries he had seen. So, I wrote a very long letter to my mother in Illinois and told her to pass it around to all our friends!

The team spent most evenings in its beautiful new home, listening to the Armed Forces Network, playing bridge, and writing letters. Former T Force associates also visited us. In particular, we enjoyed seeing Ozzie Backus again, who was now with Team 96, working with the Military Government in Trier. And, Henry Schuster and I were getting to know our new teammates.

Lieutenant Kriwer at age forty-five was one of the oldest officers still serving. He had been in the Austrian Army in 1918, came to the States in the 1930s and then began his World War II service in the U.S. Quartermaster Corps.

Lieutenant Seiden had been a lieutenant in the Polish Army as late as 1938, then came to the States and began his U.S. Army service in 1942 with the 80th Infantry Division.

Sergeant Jan Polivka and his sister came to the States in the late 1930s as well, but from Czechoslovakia. Their father had been an engineer at the University of Prague. He fled with his family because of fears that the occupying Nazis would persecute Czech intellectuals. Jan was barely twenty years old when he arrived on U.S. shores.

Corporal Henry Griesman was the son of a German physician in Nuremberg. Among his patients were the families of two German Army generals. In 1938, they advised him to get out of Germany to escape the coming persecution of Jewish people. Henry said that the family packed and left within a week, settling in New York, where Dr. Griesman resumed work at his profession.

Our target raids continued and included some of the cities along the Rhine, such as Neustadt. Besides bringing back documents, Jan managed to get some Rhine wine along the way. Some days were spent just preparing reports at the division headquarters.

The photographs of those days show a country in turmoil. Trains (usually freight trains with open doors) passed by, loaded with displaced persons and workers returning to their homelands. Who could tell how many days their journeys would last, or on how many different trains they would have to travel?

And then, there were the discharged German soldiers. Surrendered troops had gone to a huge tent city in the fields along the west bank of the Rhine, between Bonn and Coblenz. From there, the farmers were released first of all, to work on their crops. They rode on the backs of every truck moving along the roads.

Their release was followed by other regular troops. However, SS commissioned and non-commissioned officers were placed into special camps for release at a later time. Much more about that will be related later on.

There was more work preparing reports at the division headquarters. Being around there offered the opportunity to catch a couple of concerts. One evening, a chorus from the division 110th Regiment entertained their audience. On another occasion, a USO variety show came to Kaiserlautern. Back at the corps headquarters, there was also a Red Cross club to visit.

Several trips were made to the Saarland, which had been heavily damaged by artillery and heavy weapons fire. A few comments about the history of that area were made earlier. It was basically an area of coal mines and steel mills. The Treaty of Versailles, which ended World War I, gave the French the use of the coal mines as reparations, though the Saarland was governed by the League of Nations. In 1935, the people there voted to elect their own parliament and to unite with Germany two years later.

The team searched targets in the capital, Saarbruecken, and in some of the other cities, like Voelklingen and St. Ingbert. However, as we began our second month in Kaiserlautern, the pace of our activities did slow down. There were a few more locations to visit, including Alzey and Worms along the Rhine. Worms is a 2,000 year old city which had witnessed a number of events involving Martin Luther and the early Protestant Church. Its central cathedral stood for all to see, undamaged by the war.

Scenery around those cities was spectacular, not only for the hills and river but also because of the vineyards and fields full of poppies. Jan and I found a photographer in Waldfischbach, southwest of Kaiserlautern who did excellent work. I recall that his pay was mainly cigarettes we purchased at the division PX exchange! However, there were no targets in that town, so the trips were not really official.

Once, when returning to Kaiserlautern on the German Autobahn, the team traveled a stretch in an easterly direction as a thunderstorm on its right paralleled its course. The end of the brightest rainbow followed the storm and moved along at the Jeep's speed. It was a breath-taking sight and most unforgettable.

Now and then, we all spent days working at the corps and division headquarters, on reports and on updating individual service records. The latter function became very important to each soldier, for a point system had been established to determine rotation to the States and subsequent discharge from the service. It was based upon the number of months served, the number of months overseas, the number of campaigns in which each soldier had served, and on service awards earned. On Team 97, Lieutenant Kriwer and Jan Polivka had accumulated the most points, and therefore expected to leave before any of the others.

On June 20, I spent the day translating for the legal personnel in the Military Government in Neustadt. A few days later, the team lent its assistance in the centers for French and Italian displaced persons near Kaiserslautern, though it was scarcely expert in the Italian language. It should be pointed out, however, that most of the displaced persons had acquired some knowledge of German.

Still, the events mentioned did not comprise a month of work in June, by any means. So, there was time to use a pass for a few days' leave. The two Henrys went to Paris in the fourth week of the month. The week before that, I visited my favorite destination—Luxembourg and Arlon, Belgium. For two days, I was a guest of the Arends, who were the uncle and aunt of Denise Muller. It was a real pleasure to enjoy their excellent meals, to take walks through the countryside and to visit both families. Denise's younger sister Helen and I even spent a couple of hours playing piano duets.

The ride to Luxembourg had been a fairly easy one, but I had to hitchhike all the way back to Kaiserslautern! It took two days, on a variety of army vehicles. The first night on the road, I found shelter at the First Battalion Headquarters of the 110th Infantry Regiment, in Saarlautern, and that worked out fine.

On June 27, the team reported both to the 12th Army Group Headquarters in Wiesbaden and then to the Military Intelligence Headquarters in Bad Schwalbach. The two Henrys were still on their trip to France but at both locations, Jan and I had the pleasure of encountering old friends—Ozzie Backus at the first and Charles Herndon at the second one. We invited Ozzie to spend the next weekend in Kaiserslautern. All had a great time, eating, drinking wine and playing bridge. That's right—bridge was sometimes the principal leisure activity.

On July 5, the team learned that the 28th Division was leaving Kaiserslautern, to return to the States. Whether or not it would then have to serve in the Pacific War was a big question mark. Hopefully not, considering all the combat it had already seen. French forces took its place occupying the Rhineland-Palatinate on July 10. Two days later, Team 97 also left for a new destination. They had said all of their good-byes, not forgetting the Military Government detachment that had treated them so hospitably. In addition, Lieutenant Colonel Hurwitz, the G-2 of the 28th Division, gave each man a copy of the letter of commendation he had written, praising the efforts of the team during the two months it had spent with them.

The new destination was a town in the center of the centrally located German province of Hesse. There, they would carry out their final assignment before some members returned to civilian life in the States.

8

July and August in Hesse

The journey in our two Jeeps on July 11 took Team 97 to Bad Schwalbach, where it stopped briefly at the MIS headquarters, visited with a few friends, and then drove on through Limburg to Marburg. In general, we were traveling in a northeasterly direction from Kaiserslautern, for a total of 125 miles.

On the following morning, we continued the trip another twenty-five miles, to the resort and spa town of Bad Wildungen. There, the 23rd Corps headquarters directed us to the small nearby country town of Gellershausen. It had a farm population of about 300 persons and an untold number of geese. It was also extremely proud of its 700-year-old church on top of a hill in the valley. The team stayed in a private home for the next three nights and had meals with a nearby CIC detachment.

In addition, the headquarters of the 3rd Infantry Division, which occupied the surrounding area, was also nearby. It had earned the unfortunate reputation of being the hardest-hit division in the war.

The next day found a couple of the team servicing our trusty Jeeps, under the watchful eye of Jan Polivka. Their reward was a swim in the nearby Eder See the following day. That lake, incidentally, had a dam which the British had taken out with precision bombing during the war. They had practiced the whole operation in Scotland, minus the bombs.

The following day, July 15, we backtracked sixty miles to Weilburg on the Lahn River. There we interrogated some scientists the following day, as part of a larger effort to learn about German rocket science. That had become the hot topic at the end of the war, in place of the efforts to learn more about the V-1 and V-2 unmanned missiles that had been previously encountered in England and Belgium.

When the day was nearly over, we proceeded another twenty-five miles north to Dillenburg, where we stayed in a hotel for a few nights. We found the town, though small, to be very photogenic, located as it was on the Dill River at the eastern edge of the Westerwald (Western Forest, north of Frankfurt). Jan and I got a number of very nice camera shots. One, of an organ grinder, surprised us when we learned that his presence had been forbidden by the Nazis because that occupation had been judged to be begging. We also found some of the populace to be very charming. More about that shortly.

The following day, we interrogated more scientists all day long, in Dillenburg itself. Then, having worked so hard even though the war was over, we took it easy for the next three days, which were a Wednesday, Thursday and Friday.

We learned that there was a camp for Polish Army WACs (Women's Army Corps) close by. There was to be a dance on Wednesday night, so the three unmarried members of the team went there together. And, we met some very nice young ladies. They had escaped from their country in 1939, when Poland was overrun, and spent the war years in England. So, the two Henrys and I did not need to speak Polish to carry on a conversation.

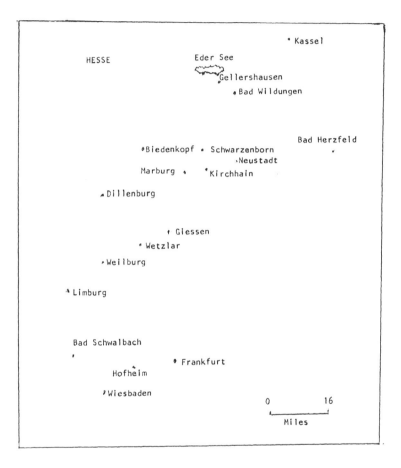

HESSE

Kassel

Eder See
Gellershausen
Bad Wildungen

Bad Herzfeld

Biedenkopf Schwarzenborn
Neustadt
Marburg Kirchhain

Dillenburg

Giessen
Wetzlar
Weilburg

Limburg

Bad Schwalbach

Hofheim
Frankfurt

Wiesbaden

0   16
Miles

107

The evening was so much fun, that we met them again the next day, for a Jeep ride through the pretty, hilly countryside and some marvelous photo-taking. Having photographs that could be looked at over and over again in future years always brought one question to my mind. That was, did the WACs ever get back to their homeland during the ensuing years of Communist rule? Or did the rulers there deny them a return because of their exposure to a democratic society in England? It's a fair question, but we shall probably never know the answer.

I even saw my favorite WAC, Sofia, again on Friday—but then came Saturday, when we had to return to work to earn our pay. The team participated in a U.S. Army census-taking of displaced persons still residing in Germany. That job was the second reason it had come to Dillenburg. Saturday's effort was to scour the town to locate and register any displaced persons, but only a few were found.

Sunday was even busier, so the work week had become quite inverted, it seemed. Some of the team drove south fifty miles to Hofheim, near Frankfurt, to assist in establishing a road block system to register displaced persons who were on the move. It was an all-day job, so we stayed with a nearby medical battalion overnight, and drove back to Dillenburg the next morning.

With the census behind us, our duties seemed to be completed, other than the usual maintenance on the Jeeps. So, we spent most of the week on leisure activities. The Polish WACs had their weekly dance again on Wednesday, and that was most enjoyable.

On Sunday, July 29, we returned to the Bad Wildungen area and settled into a small, spotless resort hotel in Gellershausen for the next month. Some had physical exams the next day. Then, on Tuesday, July 31, Henry Schuster and I began a long stretch of essential office duty for the 23rd Corps, in the Corps CIC office located in a house in Bad Wildungen. We actually moved in there, leaving the hotel in Gellershausen.

The office work began with payroll preparation. There were twelve or more teams which had been attached to the 23rd Corps by the MIS, With six persons each, that meant a payroll of seventy-two people or more. It's not certain why I had been selected to do that work, but perhaps the reason was that I had received payroll training after finishing my basic training in North Carolina, while I was awaiting my next assignment. As for Henry, I was now supposed to be training him!

We two got into the habit of spending our evenings in Gellershausen, socializing with Helga Schwagereit, her parents and occasionally with Hannelore and her other friends. Helga had helped out with the housekeeping in the private home where the team stayed when we first arrived in Gellershausen.

Helga was only sixteen, so she was sort of the little sister neither Henry or I had ever had! Her parents had moved to town in order to escape the bombing around their hometown, which was Velbert, another suburb of Essen not far from Kettwig. Her father, Hugo Schwagereit, had a plumbing supply business there which proved to be a most successful venture as Germany rebuilt itself in the ensuing years. Beyond that, the Schwagereit family became lifelong friends of my family, even to this day, both because of the association in Gellershausen and also because they subsequently became acquainted with my relatives in Kettwig.

On August 7, a remarkable event occurred to me. My service record, which had gone astray after I had left England, finally reappeared. The large envelope which transmitted it, which I still have today, had all kinds of forwarding addresses on it. First of all, it had gone to the 82nd Airborne Division. I never served with a team there, of course, and a search of the division's directory revealed that. Then, it was sent from unit to unit around the theater of operations—in which order it is impossible to discern. Finally, it was forwarded to MII Team 499-G, with which I was not yet affiliated! But I would be, in the next assignment.

So, without a service record, I had never received any pay and was virtually out of cash. However, that was not as serious as it sounds, for a couple of reasons. First, in a combat zone, there was no charge for supplies from the PX exchange, such as toiletries, candy, some food, cigarettes, minor clothing, pocket books and so on. Secondly, as has been indicated, even when I had to pay someone, such as a photo developer, I often resorted to barter, using PX supplies. Anyway, the problem was solved when I cut myself a payroll check for all the back pay a couple of days later!

After that, Henry and I got into some highly interesting work. The results were eagerly awaited by all the personnel. A point system, referred to earlier, had been devised for determining the order of returning to the States. It worked like this: one point for each month of service to date, another point for each month spent overseas and five points for each military campaign or special award received.

The two of us then consulted long listings which included all units that had participated in the five military campaigns of the 12th Army Group. They were: Normandy, from June to August, Northern France from then to December; the Ardennes from then to February; the

Rhineland from then to March, and Central Europe thereafter. Whenever we found a team listed for a campaign, we made a notation in each soldier's service record.

Following that, we computed a point total for each soldier. Each soldier was given his total and had a chance to make corrections. My total, for example, was sixty-eight points, while Jan Polivka's was eighty two. Obviously, he was going back home first, and he did.

About the same time, everyone received the new uniform jacket, the so-called Eisenhower ETO blouse. It made us look a lot trimmer as we did our work each day or visited the local Red Cross Club in the late afternoon or evening. We all enjoyed that, and occasionally ran into some old acquaintances at the club, such as Herbert Haas of Team 95, who had also been at the MIC in the fall.

While Henry and I were doing all the tasks mentioned above, the rest of our Team 97 was roving about, visiting some overlooked target sites and other former installations. Meanwhile, atomic bombs had been dropped in Japan, and everyone knew the war was about to end. Then the announcements came, and several days of celebration started on August 14. To participate in that, Henry and I decided to join a truckload of soldiers from the 23rd Corps for a three day pass in Brussels.

It turned out to be an eleven-hour ride each way, and rain fell all day long, both going and returning. However, the three days in Brussels (August 16 through 18) were delightful. And the city went wild. Brussels was the principal headquarters for the British Armies on the continent, and all those service people knew then that they would not have to face re-deployment to the Pacific theater. Of course, all American troops were equally happy about that, such as the soldiers in the 3rd Infantry Division, which had endured so much.

In Brussels, everyone did all kinds of activities, such as visiting several different night clubs for service people, taking a bus tour of the city, seeing an exhibit of G.I. art in a fancy art gallery and taking lots of photographs. To say nothing of just mingling with the happy crowds!

However, I did attempt to accomplish one thing while I was there. My friend Anne Manning, from the days at the MIS headquarters in Broadway, England, had a sister Kay who was serving with a British unit in Brussels. I spent a half day searching for her and did find her unit, but she had just been transferred elsewhere.

Something more should be said about Anne herself, relating another wartime story with its tragic overtones. I had met her at a dance in Broadway one evening. Soon, I learned that she was engaged to an RAF pilot whose plane had been lost over France just before D-Day. Nevertheless, we did become friends, and she even invited me to her parents' home in Birmingham to celebrate my 21st birthday on August 20, 1944.

Her fiance, Dennis Hargreaves, had piloted the airplane on a Special Operations flight, dropping three agents in France. On the return trip, the aircraft came under anti-aircraft fire and crashed near the small town of Longue in the Loire Valley. All five crew members were lost, and are buried near the crash site. However, the British Intelligence Service suppressed all information about that event for seven more years, which would seem to any reasonable person to be an inexcusable action.

Anne attended the University of Birmingham, training to be a teacher. There she met Derrick Mitchell, a veteran of the war in Asia who was taking the same courses. They were married and have remained lifelong friends of my family whom we have visited with great enjoyment on our periodic trips abroad.

When Henry and I returned to Bad Wildungen on August 19, we learned that scarcely two weeks remained in our service there. The whole group there had a marvelous, surprise birthday party for my 22nd birthday the very next day. Cards, a cake, flowers—the works—helped, of course, by the four marvelous Germans who prepared both meals and quarters. Then, it was back to the payrolls and service record maintenance and visiting our good friends in Gellershausen nearly every evening.

On Sunday, the team made a highly interesting trip to visit the Palace of the Prince of Waldeck in Arolsen, only fifteen miles north of us. Just two days later, Lieutenant Kriwer left to return to the States, and the rest of us realized that the team's days were numbered.

The Brussels photographs were developed and printed, with great results, and I used some of my new cash to purchase a camera case. I moved back to the private home that had first provided rooms for the team in Gellershausen, so I could be near our German friends.

On September 1, the team again visited a former ordnance depot just north of Bad Wildungen. Then we got ready to report to our new headquarters, namely, the G-2 Section of the 7th U.S. Army in Heidelberg, on September 5.

Before that, there was still a most important personal mission to accomplish. When I had first written my mother that I was in the Bad Wildungen area, she answered that she herself had spent a few days at that spa and resort town in her girlhood. And, beyond that, she wrote me that my father's mother had come from a town named Biedenkopf twenty-five miles to the southeast, and that there were still some relatives to visit there.

So, on Sunday, September 2, I borrowed a Jeep and drove there. It was a pretty ride through the hilly countryside, and I quickly found the family I wanted to see—the Kreutzers.

Mr. Kreutzer, the brother of my paternal grandmother Auguste, greeted me, along with his wife and two daughters, Ellie and Erna. All were most charming people, and I was so glad to get some photos of them. Ellie was a nurse, and Erna had been the wife of a man who operated a coal mine. She took me to see her beautiful home, where another surprise awaited me.

She had some soldiers living in her home, and I found one of them to be Jack Altbaum, who had trained at Camp Ritchie with me the year before. He was serving with one of the CIC (Counter Intelligence Corps) teams in that area. After chatting with him, I left him with the instructions to behave himself in the home of my first cousin once removed! What a small world it was!

Back at the Kreutzer home, the visit went on a little while longer. Erna's brother Julius had not made an appearance that day. He was a cousin of my father who had often played in soccer games with him. Now, he was awaiting his discharge from the German Army, where he had been a colonel, and the family was expecting his arrival any day. I said that I would make another visit if possible and meet him then.

The visit was all too short, but I had to return to Bad Wildungen. Two days later, the five remaining members of Team 97 drove south. We did stop for lunch at Dillenburg. Then we stayed in a suburb of Frankfurt for the night. On the next day, Wednesday, September 5, we reported to the G-2 Section of the 7th Army in Heidelberg.

9

Two More Months in Hesse with a New Team

In Heidelberg, the famous German university city on the Neckar River, the 7th Army headquarters complex was in a large cluster of German Army barracks. Team 97 went straight to the G-2 Section, where it encountered lots of old friends and acquaintances from Camp Ritchie and from other teams in the MIS.

In all, ten teams, including 97, were released from service with the 23rd Corps of the 15th Army and attached to the 7th Army, which would be occupying a large portion of southern Germany. Team 97 was disbanded, with Lieutenant Paul Seiden, Sergeant Jan Polivka and Corporal Henry Griesman facing early re-deployment to the States. Henry Schuster and I, on the other hand, were assigned to MII (Military Intelligence Interpretation) teams, which usually worked with the Military Government. Henry went to Team 534-G, and I was attached to Team 499-G. So, we said our good-byes and parted with the associates we had worked with both at T Force and in the activities after V-E Day.

The new teammates were mainly more recent graduates from Camp Ritchie, and some had not participated at all in the military operations before D-Day. They included Captain Charles Marshall, Sergeant Harvey

Tebrich, Sergeant Ernest Stern, Sergeant Rudolf Kaufman and Corporal Kurt Lowenthal, plus myself. Unfortunately, I no longer have a copy of the Army orders which listed the full roster of the team, so the data above may be slightly inaccurate. Nevertheless, those were the men with whom I would be associated for the next three months, on two assignments.

The same day, Wednesday, September 5, my new teammates drove me to the first location, the small town of Kirchhain. It was just east of Marburg, also a university city, about fifty-five miles north of Frankfurt. There, they had quarters in a large house, where we were nicely settled by evening. To pinpoint the location even more, it was twenty miles due east of Biedenkopf, the home of the Kreutzers, about twenty-five miles northeast of Dillenburg and twenty miles south of Bad Wildungen. Naturally, I was hoping to see my friends in those places again!

Work began the next morning, comprised of duties unlike any I had seen before. Team 499 and two others formed a CIC detachment whose job it was to administer an internment camp for certain German soldiers still prisoners of war. There were 2,000 internees in all, of which 700 were former SS troops, whose release dates had not yet been determined, and 218 were German Army generals. That group was not necessarily considered to pose a security problem like the SS troops, but they did have to be debriefed by U.S. Army historians before they could be released. During the two months the team spent at the camp, which coincidentally was called Camp 97, not much progress seemed to be made in carrying out the interviews.

The balance of the internees, almost 1,100 men, were being released as instructions came down from SHAEF.

Of course, one had to be certain of each internee's status, so he could be properly released when orders arrived.

From the photographs taken, it is obvious that the camp did not have the permanent type of German Army barracks buildings seen in so many cities. The buildings there were wooden and unpainted, like barracks that had been used by the Germans for housing foreign workers. Security fencing had been added, along with security towers and a triple security gate. The team administrative office was located in one of the buildings.

There, it kept files on each internee. I did a lot of typing of weekly operation reports, special reports, rosters of internees being released or shipped elsewhere and so on. There were constant interrogations concerning internees' status to be carried out and then written and typed.

The team drew its own rations from the Quartermaster Corps and had employed some Germans to cook the meals at the house. Usually, the work week was five-and-a-half days long, leaving Saturday afternoons and Sundays free. The occupying infantry troops in the area also had movies several evenings a week, which all were welcome to attend. They always showed the latest Hollywood movies, too.

On September 9, the first Sunday in Kirchhain, I attended a church service in the nearby town of Neustadt, where I ran into my old friend Howard Irwin. He invited me to his own quarters for dinner. That evening, I drove to another nearby town named Schwarzenborn to see Henry Schuster. His team was working there, at Camp 96.

In the next week, I drove Ernie Stern to Schwarzenborn to see the medics. While there, I saw Henry again, along with another old friend from Camp Ritchie, Ed Reynolds. Then, though it was only Thursday,

117

I decided to drive to Bad Wildungen. After all, it was only about twenty miles away. I visited the Schwagereits and stayed overnight, returning to Kirchhain for work the following morning.

The next week and a half were busy, with the team performing lots of interrogations. The main diversion was evenings of playing bridge. Team 499 was very good at that, I soon found out, as it went on for the entire fall season.

On Sunday, September 23, I took my new teammate Rudy Kaufman, who hailed from St. Louis, with me to visit the Schwagereits, just for the day. They really liked him, as everyone did.

Another busy week ensued. When Sunday arrived, I drove to Bad Wildungen again. It would be the last time for a couple of weeks. After visiting some of the men still at the 23rd Corps headquarters, like Jack Fox, I saw my friends in Gellershausen and stayed overnight.

In the next week, I took another officer to see Camp 96 in Schwarzenborn, where Henry worked. Then, just a couple days later, Ernie Stern and I had an errand in Marburg, where we had enough time to see the old university and photograph a bit.

On Sunday, October 7, I made my second visit to Biedenkopf (or Biedenhead, as the G.I.s called it). There, I saw both Erna and her parents, but Julius was still not released from the German Army. That would probably require yet another visit, if time could be found.

In the following week, I had dinner with Henry Schuster one evening, and then I had the first visit from a member of the Army's Historical Section. He was Sergeant Leonard Beck, who hailed from the Bronx in New York City. He told of the plans being made to interview all the German general prisoners, and I responded that it was high time to get going with that! I then drove him thirty miles to the east, to Bad Hersfeld, the next day. After that, I visited the Schwagereits in Gellershausen overnight again.

Two days later, on Tuesday, October 16, I received word to come to Biedenkopf, for Julius Kreutzer had returned home. I received the afternoon off and drove to Erna's home first of all, for dinner with the CIC detachment there. That included seeing Jack Altbaum again. After that, I proceeded to the Kreutzer home for my third visit.

Julius was one of the most bitter persons I have ever met, though he was cordial enough toward me, the son of his first cousin. The experience that had caused his bitterness was one more of the tragedies of the long war.

He had had to supervise the emigration of millions of Germans from East Prussia, which Germany would later lose to Poland and the USSR. Thousands perished as they were driven from their homes on foot, with only a few possessions on their backs. And when they did arrive in Germany, extreme measures had to be undertaken to find housing for them in a country which had lost so many buildings in air raids.

I have always thought that the expulsion of all those persons has been downplayed or ignored altogether by the press and by historians because of all the suffering the Nazis themselves had inflicted upon others. The exodus was not unlike one that occurred in 1939, when the Russians expelled 2,000,000 Poles from their homes and sent them to Siberia. Of course, many also perished along the way or later in the inhospitable climate of Siberia. Again, there was not the criticism that the Germans received, probably because that action had been committed by one of the U.S. Allies and not by its enemies. So much for politicizing!

On the following day, Wednesday, October 17, the team learned that Camp 97 was going to be shut. Many of the original 2,000 internees had already been released, but the team immediately began to prepare rosters of those that would be transferred to another camp. That took several more days, on into the next week, as a matter of fact. On Sunday, I made what turned out to be my next-to-last visit to Gellershausen. I was going to miss those friends!

On October 24, I drove to Marburg to see my friend Sergeant Cliff Landwer at the 3rd Replacement Division. The following day, everyone packed food and fuel and started to check out of the office at the camp. I made a brief final visit to see Henry Schuster. Then, Rudy Kaufman again accompanied me for the last visit to Gellerhausen that evening to say my good-byes.

After two more days of packing and final errands in Marburg, the team left Kirchhain at 0800 hours on October 28 and headed south to its new assignment.

**Sergeants Jack Fox and Henry
Stern, MII Team 538**

**Gellershausen near Bad Wildungen, where we
had quarters. Note 700-year-old church**

View from the church

Resort hotel where we lived

Main Street of town

Jan Polivka working

Our cook, Frau Wahl

Frau Wahl and the rest of the staff

Dillenburg, Hesse where we spent 7/16/1945 to 7/29/1945 for operation Tallyho, a census of Germany

The organ grinder, forbidden by the Nazis, returns

The plaque high on the tree reads in German: Under this linden tree the Dutch Emissaries were received by William the Silent on 4/14/1568

Wilhelmsturm

Polish WACs at their camp by Dillenburg—Alla, Karl, Sofia, Henry S., and Christine

**Back to Gellerhausen—
the Schwagereit family**

On the road to Biedenkopf

Biedenkopf—the Kreutzer home

The Kreutzers (Karl's great-uncle and aunt) with daughters Ellie and Erna

Pass to Brussels 8/15/1945 to 8/19/1945, V-J weekend. This is the leave hotel for GIs at Rue 11 Novembre.

Karl and Henry

Two GIs and Karl with gendarme

Grand Place

Karl at the Tomb of the Unknown Soldier

Henry at Manneken Pis

Returning by truck, at the German-Dutch border

Cologne's railroad station by the cathedral

Captain Charles Marshall of Team 499 with Rudi, a PW, at the Internment Camp at Kirchhain, near Marburg

7th Army Internment Camp 97 had 2,000 internees, including 700 SS men and 218 German generals.

Sergeant Howard Irwin and fans, just before he left
Kirchhain for his trip home

The 1,000-year-old town of Amoeneburg on a high
mound near Kirchhain

**Ulm's 528-foot cathedral, the world's tallest, stands alone in the bombed city
Central**

7th Army HQ at Heidelberg

Ike at HQ ceremony there

Color Guard at ceremony

Old tower bridge and transient hotel (right)

Heidelberg on the Neckar River

The 1,000-year-old castle

Scenes of the 11/25/1945 visit to the Black Forest with Kurt Lowenthal, the day before leaving for home

St. Georgen

Triberg—the Cuckoo Clock city

With Joe and Tiny   **With Harvey Franck**

Voyage home on the Liberty Ship, *John Sullivan,* leaving Bremerhaven on 12/27/1945 and arriving in New York Harbor on 1/12/1946. There were 650 men aboard, made up of the 3rd Battalion, 175th Regiment, 29th Division.

The Army's welcome yacht at New York Harbor

Pier 15—Staten Island.
Amen!

**Team 97—3rd Reunion
San Francisco—2000**

(Left to Right) Karl W. Abt, Jan Polivka, Henry Griesman, Paul Seiden, Walter Waller, Henry Schuster. White Caps from Normandy's 50th Anniversary in 1994.

(Left to right) Theza Griesman, Sandy Schuster, Judy Seiden, Jan's sister Elizabeth, and Donna Abt

10

November on the Danube

Team 499 was on its way to Ulm on the Danube, where it would administer the 7th Army's Camp 80. The journey on the Autobahn system led through Frankfurt, then past Mannheim, Karlsruhe and Stuttgart. After that, the final stretch to Ulm went through the Swabian Alps. The total drive was just over 200 miles. At its end, the team was assigned to a large house, in which it got settled most comfortably.

Ulm in those days was a city of under 75,000 inhabitants. It was situated mostly on the south bank of the Danube, which is not a very wide river that far west. It is also about sixty-five miles west of Munich, though that city is not on the Danube. Ulm claims the world's tallest church spire on its beautiful cathedral, which was built in the late 14th century. It is 528 feet high, just a few feet more than the one at Cologne.

The principal activities in Ulm have to do with commerce for the surrounding area. There is little industry that was involved with defense production. Nevertheless, the whole central business district had been destroyed in air raids. Only the cathedral had been spared. It rose more prominently than ever amid all the rubble.

The Germans called the destruction a retaliation act for what the Germans themselves had done to other nations earlier in the war, when they ruled the skies. That could be true.

Now, something about Camp 80. It was located in some of the permanent-type German Army barracks. They housed 700 to 800 commissioned and non-commissioned SS prisoners whom SHAEF had not yet scheduled for release. That was the class of prisoners that would be released last of all and then only after German local and state government posts had been staffed with other, less precarious and less risky persons. Releases did not occur in the brief month I served there and probably did not happen until well into 1946. In my opinion, and it was shared by many others, it was a wise move, for it removed that element from any influence in the future German government.

Obviously, one had to screen each prisoner very carefully. Then, when SHAEF sent an order to release all combat platoon sergeants, for example, those would be the ones to go. And not a master sergeant or a second lieutenant. Furthermore, one had to know enough about each man so that none of them could switch his identity on us. German soldiers always carried their service records with them, unlike our forces (remember my lost service record). So, the team's record of each of them had to contain the vital, identifying data in his service record.

It took a couple of days after arriving to get settled and organized. There were some repairs that had to be made to the Jeeps which required expertise beyond the team's, and there were plenty of errands to run. By the 31st of October, the office was set up and running. It had been decided that it would be in the house for the initial days and weeks, until we could be certain about the security in the barracks.

The first courier run to the 7th Army headquarters in

Heidelberg fell to me, the next day. That involved retracing the trip just finished, driving east and north about 110 miles, half of that through the Swabian Alps. The city was located between Karlsruhe and Mannheim. And someone had to go there each week to draw rations and collect mail. I stayed at the Hollaender Hof, a well known hotel near the Tower Bridge over the Neckar River. The 7th Army utilized it for transient personnel like me. That evening, I visited the local Red Cross Club, and the next morning, I took lots of photographs around the city before returning to Ulm.

One humorous incident that occurred on that day is something I've never forgotten. Up on a high hill, I took some photographs of the ruins of the Heidelberg Castle. A German worker was mowing lawn nearby, and I asked him why the castle was in ruins although none of rest of the city was. Disdaining my ignorance, he informed me that the damage to the castle had occurred in the Napoleonic Wars, 150 years ago!

The team again observed a five-and-one-half day work week, as it had in Kirchhain. The next day was Saturday, so some took the opportunity to watch an American football game in the afternoon. A team from the 101st Airborne Division played another one from the 1st Armored Division. The paratroopers won the match thirty two to zero.

On Sunday, I carried out a search all day long. Dillingen on the Danube, near where my college fraternity brother Tom Cartmell had crashed in his fighter plane on April 26th, lay only twenty miles northeast of Ulm. I spent most of the day, scouring the environs to ask farmers if they knew where the crash site was located. All pleaded ignorance of the event, or possibly, they knew but would not tell. I returned to Ulm without any success.

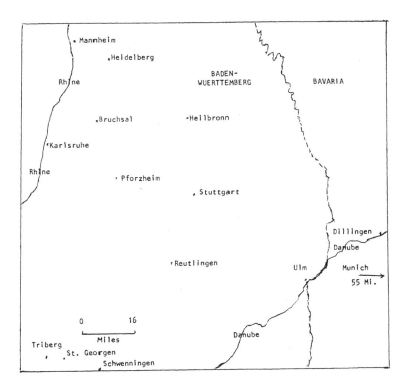

Years were to pass before I saw Tom's grave in an American cemetery in the French province of Lorraine.

The next week brought more work on the prisoner records, involving both interrogations and writing. There was also a weekly report of activities and some necessary correspondence with 7th Army headquarters late in the week. However, it was all far from boring. Some of us visited the local Red Cross Club at least twice, saw the USO musical production of *Panama Hattie*, and also watched the Williams Circus perform on Saturday afternoon. Not to mention the weekly bridge evening at the house.

The Sunday that weekend, which fell on November 11, the World War I Armistice Day, did bring a little duty. I monitored the church services at the camp and found everything to be in order. I was happy to learn that some of the tough inmates did have some religious feelings after all!

Another week of work on records and report writing began, with the usual diversions of visits to the Red Cross Club and Thursday evening bridge. Late in the week, I was offered a furlough to England so I could visit my English friends. However, I decided to turn it down, since I really expected to be sent home shortly.

On Thursday, I had a most unusual experience. One of my teammates, driving through Ulm, had spotted an *Abt Eisenwaren Laden* (Abt Hardware Store). So, I drove there alone and entered to find only one clerk working. When I asked for the proprietor, I was told that he was home recuperating from illness. I asked if it was possible to see him, since we might be relatives.

The clerk picked up the telephone and reached Herr Abt at home. I was invited to come right over and given the directions. It was a memorable visit. I told him that I came from a large clan of Abts in the Ruhr Valley, but knew that there were some elsewhere as well. Herr Abt said that was true, because there was the smaller clan around Ulm in the province of Baden-Wuerttemberg and another in Kassel in the province of Hesse, near Bad Wildungen. We two guessed that we were not related. Years later, I found another Abt in St. Louis whose family had come from the clan near Ulm.

The following weekend was also memorable. At the Red Cross Club on Saturday afternoon, I ran into my roommate from the days at Princeton—Bob Wehmhoefer! A life-long resident of New York City, he had also been a student in the German Area and Language Program at Princeton for just one semester in late 1943. At the end of that semester, both of us were tested and deemed to be proficient enough to begin intelligence training at Camp Ritchie. That said, I learned that Bob had been serving with a military government detachment since August 1944.

The next day, I saw Bob again bright and early and then left with Ernie Stern to spend the day in Munich. There we saw Keith Crim, who had been with an intelligence team in the 7th Army all along and had exchanged letters with me from time to time. After some sightseeing, we attended the first operatic presentation of the Munich Opera Company. The Company had chosen Beethoven's *Fidelio,* which has a strong freedom theme and was therefore deemed to be appropriate for reemerging Germany.

Then, guess what! At the end of the performance, our Jeep was missing, even though we had removed a vital part from the distributor. We found our way to the nearest MP station run by the 3rd Army, where it had been towed. We got it back, of course, but along with a ticket because no one had remained with the vehicle! When asked if someone of us should have missed the performance in order to baby-sit the Jeep, the MPs said yes. Anyway, upon returning to Ulm, we gave the ticket to Captain Marshall, who laughed and tore it up. So much for the red tape at Patton's 3rd Army, which had previously stopped me in Verdun for not wearing a necktie in combat!

While mentioning the Jeeps, the reader will note several photos of Ernie and me driving one named Ban Day. That name goes back to Camp Ritchie. The Commander, General Banfill, believed our country should never take each Sunday off, as it had on Pearl Harbor Day. So, all were given every eighth day off, which then rotated through the weeks, falling first on Sunday, then on Monday in the next week and so on. That eighth day was very appropriately called Ban Day!

In the next week, the office was moved into the camp, which was now believed to have sufficient security. It's possible, too, that the prisoners had come to realize that the team was there to serve their best interests during their confinement and not to make things more onerous for them.

On Tuesday, I made a second courier run to Heidelberg, returning the same day in foggy weather. Driving through the mountains turned out to be very tricky. However, I stopped at Bruchsal north of Karlsruhe to enjoy a meal with Lt. Gerhard Grieb's Team 88 there.

Thursday was Thanksgiving Day, a week early during the war years because of President Roosevelt's controversial decision to advance it. All enjoyed the food, the leisure time, the bridge playing and visiting the Red Cross Club.

My orders to return home with the 100th Infantry Division arrived the next day. Both Rudy and I would be leaving Ulm on Monday, November 26th. So, I would be leaving the team I had worked with for the last three months. I started to pack my things, but one last weekend trip remained.

On Sunday, Kurt Lowenthal and I drove to the Black Forest in extreme southwestern Germany. Actually, it wasn't really black, even though that is an exact translation of the German name, *der Schwarzwald*. It did consist of large stands of dark pine trees all over its hills and valleys, but maybe the name Dark Forest just would not have been accepted.

We drove through towns with names like Tuttlingen, Schwennigen and St. Georgen. In the small town of Triberg, which lay deep in a valley, we found a shop that made and sold cuckoo clocks. The owner sort of warmed up to his American visitors and showed us the back room, where he kept his finest clocks. Each of us bought a couple with money and coffee. We had to hustle to get them packed for mailing before leaving the next day.

And then the departure day arrived—Monday, November 26th.

11

The Long, Long Way Home

The orders to leave requested Rudy Kaufman and me to proceed to one of the companies in the 100th Infantry Division, which was located in Pforzheim between Stuttgart and Karlsruhe. One of our teammates drove us there and then bade us a safe and quick journey home. Both of us were fairly certain we could achieve the first part of that farewell wish but were a bit unsure about the second portion. And, our doubts were justified.

The next day we learned that those who had not been serving with the 100th Division but had just been added to it could leave the following day to join the 29th Division. That unit was already near the port in Bremen and was expected to sail sooner than the 100th. So, we two left at 0700 November 28 and spent many hours on railway coaches, heading north through Mannheim, Frankfurt and Fulda. The night was spent on the train, which then proceeded on through Hanover to Bremen. We were assigned to Company M of the 175th Regiment of the division and given some comfortable quarters in Worpswede, just north of the city. Tired from the two-day journey, we soon passed out that night.

Processing began the very next day, which was Friday, and was continued Saturday morning. In the evening, we visited a very fine Red Cross Club in Bremen.

The city itself, which was over 1,100 years old, had a half million inhabitants and many museums and institutions. It was located on the Weser River. More than twenty miles north of it, at the mouth of the Weser River estuary, was Bremerhaven, a quarter the size of Bremen, which had docks and fishing facilities. Only Hamburg to the east was a larger port. Rebuilding of Bremen to erase the damage of devastating air raids was already underway. We soon saw that we were going to enjoy Bremen's attractions in the few days we had to wait for passage to the States.

We took it easy on Sunday. There was a church service, of course, but then I wrote letters, read and took in the Hollywood movie of the day. After that, the new week began. The division's top officers did not want to see any idle soldiers about. There were group calisthenics, lectures and additional processing. I even had to serve for one day as the company CQ (Charge of Quarters) on Friday (thanks, no doubt, to having a few stripes on my uniform). One evening there was a bridge game and on another evening, a dance for the Third Battalion (where did non-fraternization go?).

That weekend was even busier than the previous one. We visited the Red Cross Club twice, attended church, had a wonderful dinner at the Country Club and heard a band concert Sunday evening.

In the second full week, the division's officers had more plans for everyone. To the calisthenics they added a hike and two road marches, not to mention a lecture and one inspection. That was beginning to make it seem like being in the Army! However, Monday evening brought a performance of Verdi's opera *Il Trovatore* at the Red Cross Club, followed by a concert of the Bremen Philharmonic Orchestra three days later.

It was just too much for me, for I was ill all the next weekend. On Monday, I was sent to the hospital in Bremen for a chest x-ray before being declared well again. Well enough for a road march on Tuesday, it was decided.

That week also brought another inspection, one more day as a CQ and two lectures. Guess who gave the second one? None other than yours truly! I was asked to discuss current events. Resources were not very plentiful, compared to what there is today. There was the army's newspaper, *The Stars and Stripes*, which was published each day. The edition for Germany was published in Frankfurt and usually consisted of eight pages, tabloid size. Then, there were the daily broadcasts of the Armed Forces Network. Finally, I had a subscription to *Time* magazine, given by a friend at home. This was a miniature magazine which was folded and mailed in a business-size envelope. I don't remember from where, but it came quite regularly. It was called the "Pony Edition."

So, I did my best, using all of the above resources. I must have done an acceptable job, for I was asked to do the same later on the troopship. Incidentally, the day of lecture, December 21, was the day General Patton died, after being injured in a car/truck accident. However, that news was not available before the lecture.

Years later, my wife and I saw his grave in a military cemetery near the city of Luxembourg. At that point, I no longer harbored any resentment about the cavalier treatment his MPs had twice shown me. General Patton was one of the greatest.

The weekend before Christmas brought another visit to the Country Club in Bremen and church, of course. On Monday, which was December 24, some of us visited the Red Cross Club and then had dinner at the Country Club, before seeing a performance of Bayer's *Fairy Doll* ballet.

On Christmas Day there was a German church service in Worpswede, which those who knew the language attended. Then, we had an excellent army dinner and some played bridge, before receiving the most wonderful gift. The ship would leave the very next day!

A train took everyone to the port of Bremerhaven, where we had to undergo some processing, of course. The next day, the train again took us to the dock, where we boarded a Liberty ship named the *John Sullivan*. There were 650 men in all—the entire third battalion of the 175th Infantry Regiment. That also included a few like me who had been assigned to the unit only for the trip home.

Today, one flies from New York to Germany in about seven hours. Compare that to the journey ahead, which lasted sixteen days!

Sailing time was 1645 hours on December 27. The ship proceeded through the English Channel, where it encountered a storm and actually lay at anchor near Rotterdam on the following evening.

On December 28, I was again asked to give a current events talk over the public address system, that day. Then, a couple of days later, the seas were calm again, and the Sunday church service was held on deck. Everyone saw Land's End in England, and then encountered another day-long storm on December 30. On January 1, 1946, of all things, I gave another current events talk over the public address system, the third one in the past month.

Two days later, I came down with a severe case of influenza. My temperature was over 103 degrees, and I was actually in a semi-conscious state for much of the time. Penicillin was administered, but I don't know how effective that was. Apparently, the doctor was even concerned

157

about my survival, for he found a lieutenant from Evanston, Illinois to speak with me. That was done so that he could meet later with my mother, if I didn't survive. I was conscious enough to figure out that much.

The illness lasted for ten days, until the ship reached New York harbor on January 12. Then I rallied some, and was able to get up and watch the noisy reception given the *John Sullivan*. And you'll never guess what each soldier was given on the dock, after the landing. It was a bottle of fresh milk! Apparently, the Army had learned that was one item that almost everyone had missed while overseas.

A train took everyone to Camp Kilmer, New Jersey the same day. I was just able to telegraph my arrival to my mother and then suffered a relapse. This time, I spent three days in a private room and was then placed in a ward for the next eight days. I managed to write and telegraph home and also received two letters from there. Before being released from the ward on January 22, I had to have final x-rays and blood tests, of course, and even had to visit a dentist.

Just getting back into a uniform proved to be an experience, for I had lost forty pounds during my two illnesses and was down to the 130-pound range. This time, I managed to telephone home and impart my latest news. They were much relieved, of course, though I couldn't tell what they would think of their skinny soldier!

My mother had the strangest tale to tell me. She had been called by a sergeant at Camp Grant, near Rockford, Illinois, from which I was to be discharged. The sergeant wanted her to tell if she knew where her son had disappeared to! Isn't it wonderful to be missed!

During the next two days, I paid a final visit to the men still confined in the hospital ward. Also, there was a chance to look into the service club at Kilmer and see a movie. On January 24, I left for Illinois on a Pullman train car. It arrived in the Chicago train yards one day later and at Camp Grant that same evening. There was just enough time left to get settled in a barracks and telephone home.

The next morning, Saturday, January 26, greeted us with a temperature of minus five degrees. Those who had arrived the night before handed in their equipment (except for personal belongings). As it was, I no longer carried much equipment, for it had been left behind somewhere in Camp Kilmer when I suffered the relapse. The Army already had it.

Not much else happened on Saturday. There was another movie and a visit to the service club. The next morning, after church and a good dinner, processing started in earnest. Then came Monday, January 28—my final day in the service. All were counseled, signed their exit papers and attended a discharge ceremony at 1600 hours.

After that, another soldier who lived in one of the North Shore suburbs of Chicago was met by his parents, in their car. They took me along and deposited me on the doorstep of my mother's home in Wilmette at 1700 hours!

No, it wasn't V-E Day or V-J Day, but for those returning home it was the most important day of all. For, they were living, and they were loved and they were the lucky ones!

12
Where They Are Today

At the beginning of 2000, many lists were published which ranked the most important happenings of the second millennium. That occurred despite the fact that the new millennium did not actually begin until 2001. Probably, human nature just insisted it should start when the year's first digit changed. On one list, the greatest person of the millennium was Johannes Gutenberg, for his invention of the printing press and then the appearance of the first printed Bibles.

One event that was down the list from that was the discovery of the Internet. In the 1960s J.C.R. Licklider led an agency established in the Eisenhower administration called the Advanced Research Projects Agency (ARPA). That agency initiated the planning for the ARPANET, a limited-access information superhighway. During the next two decades, others expanded on that work, leading to the Internet millions now use.

In 1997, I began people searches on the Internet, using such sites as www.anywho.com and www.peoplefinder.com. My first areas of concentration were the rosters of Teams 97 and 94, as shown on U.S. Army orders I had from 1944–45. For example, I found there were nine men in the U.S. named Paul Seiden, based upon telephone listings. So, I wrote nine letters and found the one I wanted in Calabasas, California!

Others were even easier. I found five Werner Barths, two Robert Kriwers, two Henry Griesmans, three Richard Schifters and only one Morris Parloff. When each received his letter, the correct one usually telephoned immediately. Those were enthusiastic and enjoyable conversations, and an up-to-date roster was developed for each team. For a couple of men (Jan Polivka and Henry Schuster), I did not need an Internet search for I had had their addresses for years.

The men who had served on Team 97 expressed a desire in their E-Mail messages to meet again. The first reunion took place in 1998 in White Plains, New York. They were there again the next year, but then moved to San Francisco in 2000, where all six living members of the team were present, with their spouses, of course. The 2001 reunion occurred in Savannah, Georgia. Later that year, Jan Polivka died, so the 2002 reunion in Chicago brought together only five men and spouses.

The remainder of this chapter will relate some biographical details of each of the team members, including some others whose teams sometimes worked in affiliation with Teams 97 and 94.

Sergeant Oswald P. Backus III, usually called Ozzie, had served in the T Force on Team 95. His name was not on the Internet, but Oswald P. Backus IV, who was obviously his son, was there. He quickly referred me to his mother Barbara, in Lawrence, Kansas. Her E-Mail said that Ozzie had earned a Ph.D. in Russian History at Yale University after the war. He then taught at Rutgers University for two years, before moving to the University of Kansas. There he rose to the position of Director of Slavic and Soviet Area Studies. Most unfortunately, he died of heart failure in Lawrence in 1972, when he was only fifty years old.

Lieutenant Werner H. Barth lived in Salisbury, North Carolina, after a long academic career that ended in 1980. After the war, he earned a degree in modern European history from Baylor University. That was followed by a Ph.D. from the University of Texas in 1954.

Then, he taught history at Kansas State University, the University of Maryland overseas and Lock Haven University in Pennsylvania. He and his wife Jo were married in 1944 and have a family consisting of a son and daughter, four grandchildren and three great grandchildren. He died in June, 2001 at a Veterans Hospital in Salisbury. The teams remain in touch with his wife Jo and carry her name on the Team 94 roster.

Corporal Henry Griesman remained in the service after the rest, in the German Scientist Search Program. Staying in the Army Reserve, he was called back to service during the Korean War, when became an intelligence officer at Fort Bragg and then Fort Hood.

Following that, he embarked upon a long career in New York City, involved in the importing of textiles and the extensive traveling that required. He and his wife Theza have been married for more than fifty years. She has maintained an academic career with her alma mater, Connecticut College, while Henry himself is a graduate of Columbia University. They have two sons, a daughter and five grandchildren.

Lieutenant Robert Kriwer did not appear on the Internet, but his son in Delaware was there. Robert, Jr. informed us that his father had spent a long career after the war working for the Sperry Rand Corporation. Then in April, 1979, when he was seventy-eight years old, he contracted illnesses requiring hospital care. Despondent over his health, he took his own life while on his farm near Ephrata, Pennsylvania.

Lieutenant Morris Parloff resides in Bethesda, Maryland with his wife Gloria, to whom he has been married for over fifty-five years. Their family includes two sons and one grandson. Morris earned a Ph.D. in psychology and subsequently held a number of academic posts, including the University of California, the University of Maryland, Georgetown University, and American University. He is still with the Washington School of Psychiatry.

Sergeant Jan Polivka worked during the postwar years as a transportation engineer for the large municipal transport systems in California and New York. He and his wife Helen lived in West Hempstead, Long Island during their final years. They were parents of twin sons, born shortly after the war. Tom lived near them on Long Island, while John resided in a suburb of Columbus, Ohio. Helen passed away in February, 1999, and then Jan died of cancer in November, 2001, at the home of his son John. At the 2002 reunion of the team in Chicago, a memorial service was conducted for him.

Sergeant Richard Schifter and his wife Lilo also live in Bethesda, Maryland. Married for more than fifty years, they have five children, all engaged in the professions, and eight grandchildren. After his discharge from the service, he worked as a civilian in the Military Government. That was followed by degrees from the College of the City of New York and the Yale Law School. His wife is also a lawyer, and he began his own career with thirty-three years of legal practice.

After that, Dick resumed his government service as the U.S. Representative on the U.N. Human Rights Commission, then as the Deputy U.S. Representative in the

U.N. Security Council, and then as Assistant Secretary of State for Human Rights, followed by Special Assistant to the President for National Security Affairs, and now as Special Advisor to the Secretary of State. Certainly, a most distinguished career.

Corporal Henry Schuster now lives in Northbrook, Illinois, a northern suburb of Chicago. His first wife Natalie died of cancer in the 1980s. Hank is now married to Sandy, and their combined family has four children and four grandchildren. He has a degree from Northwestern University and spent much of his career in sales functions for a lighting manufacturer.

Lieutenant Paul Seiden lives in Calabasas, California, which is in the famed San Fernando Valley, north of Los Angeles. He is now married to Judy, following his first marriage. They have a combined family of four children, including two attorneys and one teacher in Italy, and four grandchildren. Paul has master's degrees from the American College in Pennsylvania in both financial service and management plus three credentials in the insurance industry. He still maintains his insurance practice in Encino, California, near his home.

I finally found Captain Benno Selcke in 2001. Following his wartime service, he worked as a government employee teaching the German language to U.S. personnel. In 1973, at the age of sixty, he retired. At first, he and his German wife lived on a farm in Alabama, which was not to her liking. They then moved to Munich and lastly to Strasbourg, where she died in 2000. Benno has returned to Anniston, Alabama.

Sergeant Walter Waller now lives in Roca Raton, Florida, after the many years he and his wife Lee spent in New York City. He received a degree in interior architecture and design from the School of Professional Art in

New York City. He then embarked upon a long career as an interior designer. Lee passed away in April, 1999, following their move to Boca Raton. They have a family of two daughters, one of them a lawyer, and three grandchildren. Always a frequent traveler to overseas destinations, Walter has continued doing just that. He makes it difficult to plan a team reunion date!

Lastly and slightly out of alphabetical order, your writer, Sergeant Karl Abt, resides in Rolling Meadows, Illinois, a northwest suburb of Chicago. My wife Donna and I, now married fifty-five years, have three children and seven grandchildren. We met as students at the Oak Park, Illinois High School. She received a degree from Beloit College in Wisconsin in 1945, but my degree from Northwestern University was delayed until 1948, when we were also married. Years later, I also received a master's degree from Roosevelt University in Chicago and became licensed as a CPA.

I spent forty-two years as a financial executive in industry. Upon retirement at the end of 1989, I opened my own CPA practice in Rolling Meadows, which I still maintain. I am also a lifelong musician, a student of the clarinet. In fact, after my Army basic training, I was offered the chance to spend my military career playing in an army band. However, I thought I would prefer the military career described in this narrative, based on my knowledge of the German language. Today, I enjoy music by playing in the very fine Community Concert Band in nearby Arlington Heights, Illinois.

That ends the biographical sketches, unless some searches now underway yield successful results. As in all military intelligence, the search goes on!